LANCASTER

OSPREY
PUBLISHING

CONTENTS

INTRODUCTION

The Lancaster is among the legendary aircraft that served the Royal Air Force during World War II.

In a letter of thanks to its manufacturer, A. V. Roe and Co., in December 1945, Commander-in-Chief of Royal Air Force Bomber Command, Sir Arthur Harris, described the Lancaster as being the greatest single factor in winning the recent conflict. He based this astonishing claim on the fact that it was responsible for dropping two-thirds of the RAF's bomb tonnage after the beginning of 1942.

The Lancaster equipped more squadrons than any other RAF bomber type, forming the backbone of Bomber Command, whose bloody war of attrition against German industry (often misunderstood and sometimes condemned) undeniably laid the foundations of the Allied victory. With a tally of ten Victoria Crosses (of the 32 'air' VCs awarded during World War II), Lancaster aircrew received more VCs than were won by the crews of any other aircraft type.

Most observers and analysts at the time, and since, agree that the aircraft was infinitely better than any of its predecessors or rivals. 'Bomber' Harris himself summarised the conventional wisdom when he baldly stated:

> One Lancaster is to be preferred to four Halifaxes. The Halifax suffers about four times the casualties for a given bomb tonnage. Low ceiling and short range make it an embarrassment when planning attacks with Lancasters.

OPPOSITE A Lancaster and Spitfire in flight over Normany on 5 June, 2014, the eve of the 70th anniversary of D-Day. (GUILLAUME SOUVANT/AFP/Getty Images)

In fact, the Lancaster actually suffered a higher loss rate than the Halifax during the daylight raids that predominated at the end of the war, and its crews were more likely to die if their aircraft was shot down. Many also suspect that the Lancaster crews, bombing from higher altitude in greater discomfort, may have been less accurate in delivering their bombs. Finally, although it carried a heavier bomb load, the Lancaster was a less useful multi-role aeroplane than the capacious Halifax, and was less well suited for tropical operations.

But in Arthur Harris's strategic bombing campaign, live aircrew in prisoner of war (PoW) camps were no more useful than the dead, and getting bombs 'bang-on' a pinpoint target was of less concern than saturating what were usually 'area targets'. Nor were the Lancaster's abilities in what Harris saw as 'secondary' roles and theatres of any great concern. The fact that the average Lancaster delivered 154 tons of bombs in its 27.2-sortie life, and could reach beyond Berlin, made it more useful than a shorter-range Halifax averaging only 100 tons. As a result, Lancasters dropped 608,612 tons of bombs out of a Bomber Command total of 955,044.

With these advantages being enjoyed by an aircraft that was also cheaper to produce, it was inevitable that the Lancaster would be built in larger numbers than any other British bomber, and would bear the brunt of the bombing campaign. They were despatched on 156,192 operational sorties during the war, and 3,836 were lost. These sorties included 107,085 in raids against Germany (23,204 by day) during which 2,508 Lancasters were lost (179 by day), representing almost half the Bomber Command total. By comparison, Halifaxes flew 47,069 sorties against Germany (10,074 by day) and suffered 1,467 losses.

But it would be wrong to suggest that the Lancaster prospered only because it met the narrow requirements of Sir Arthur Harris and his strategic bombing campaign. The Lancaster was a superb pilot's aircraft, and was preferred by most who sampled other bomber types.

The Lancaster's narrow focus and suitability for the pure bomber role was largely the result of its wartime genesis. The Halifax and Stirling had been designed in peacetime for the anticipated needs of war, whereas the Lancaster was designed in the light of real operational experience. Multi-role capability was not needed, while ease and economy of production were more important than crew comfort.

Moreover, the Lancaster and its crews also performed some of the most daring pinpoint attack missions of the war. In the end, though, it was the war of attrition waged against Germany's industrial heartland that won the conflict, and the high-profile precision attacks were relatively unimportant. In this war, the Lancaster's ability to carry a very heavy load made it of critical importance.

And if the Lancaster's widespread use, popularity, superb handling characteristics and combat record were not enough to win it a place in aviation legend, its story was one of great success dramatically grabbed from the jaws of ignominious failure – of one of the world's greatest aircraft being derived from one of the very worst.

The Lancaster entered frontline service in the early spring of 1942, and served throughout the war and even afterwards, eventually being supplanted in RAF service by the Lincoln (originally known as the Lancaster B.Mk IV). By 1945, Bomber Command included 56 Lancaster squadrons and could routinely call upon around 750 frontline aircraft, with many more serving training units, and others pouring off the production lines as attrition replacements.

The scale of its production and length of service ensures that the Lancaster's story is of epic proportions, from its earliest sorties in 1942, through the infamous Dambusters raid of May 1943 to the massive, devastating raids that eventually brought Hitler's Germany to its knees in 1945.

CHRONOLOGY

1936
July	Air Ministry issues Specification B.12/36 for a new four-engined heavy bomber.
14 Jul	RAF Bomber Command forms.
24 Aug	Specification P.13/36 issued for a new twin-engined bomber.
8 Sept	Air Ministry orders two prototypes of the Avro 679 (Manchester), designed against P.13/36.

1937
July	Air Ministry orders 200 Avro 679 bombers.

OPPOSITE Avro Lancaster bombers nearing completion at the A. V. Roe & Co. factory, Woodford, Cheshire, 6 May 1943. (Photo by Ministry of Information Official Photographer/ IWM via Getty Images)

1939
6 March	Air Ministry issues specification B.1/39 for a four-engined heavy bomber.
25 July	The Manchester flies for the first time.

1940
5 Aug	The first production Manchester is delivered.
10 Sept	First Avro Lancaster prototype ordered.
6 Nov	Manchester enters service with No. 207 Sqn.
19 Nov	Avro authorised to proceed with four prototype, four-engined Manchester III airframes.

1941
9 Jan	First flight of the initial Manchester III prototype.
24 Feb	First Manchester operation.

28 Feb	'Lancaster' name officially adopted to replace Manchester III.
31 Oct	First production Lancaster completes its first flight.
24 Dec	No. 44 Sqn receives the first three operational Lancasters.

1942

22 Feb	Air Chief Marshal Arthur Harris takes over Bomber Command.
March	Window is tested in secret.
3/4 Mar	Lancaster operations begin with No. 44 Sqn mining sorties.
10/11 Mar	No. 44 Sqn flies the first Lancaster mission over Germany.
24/25 Mar	First operational Lancaster loss.
17 April	Nos 44 and 97 Sqn Lancasters attack the Maschinenfabrik Augsburg-Nurnburg Aktiengesellschaft factory at low level.
30/31 May	First Thousand Bomber Raid, against Cologne, includes 73 Lancasters.
1/2 June	Second Thousand Bomber Raid, against Essen, includes 74 Lancasters.
24 Jun	Manchester retired from Bomber Command service.
25/26 Jun	Final Thousand Bomber Raid, against Bremen, includes 96 Lancasters.
11 Aug	Pathfinder Force established.
October	Prototype Lancaster Mk III delivered for trials. Lancaster Mk II becomes operational.

1943

30 Jan	RAF bombers begin using H2S ground-mapping radar.
5/6 March	Essen is the first target in the Battle of the Ruhr.
16 May	Nineteen No. 617 Sqn Lancasters launch to attack dams in the Ruhr estuary.
June	Monica tail-warning radar detection device introduced on Lancasters.
3/4 July	*Wilde Sau* tactics encountered for the first time.

24/25 July	Window used for the first time, during a raid on Hamburg.
13 Oct	No. 101 Sqn Lancasters introduce ABC countermeasures.
18/19 Nov	First raid of the Battle of Berlin.
23 Nov	No. 100 Group established.
3/4 Nov	Gee-H used operationally for the first time, during a raid on Dusseldorf by 344 Lancasters.

1944

9 June	No. 617 Sqn drops the Tallboy bomb operationally, against the Saumur tunnel, for the first time.
	First Lincoln prototype completes its maiden flight.
12 Nov	Nos 9 and 617 Sqn Lancasters use Tallboys to capsize *Tirpitz*.

1945

12 March	Bomber Command's largest effort of the war launches 1,108 aircraft, including 746 Lancasters, against Dortmund.
14 March	No. 617 Sqn uses Grand Slam for the first time, damaging the Bielefeld viaduct.
25 April	Lancasters fly their final offensive missions.
28 April	Lancasters begin Operation *Manna*, dropping food to the Dutch populace.
2 May	Lancasters begin flying PoWs home under Operation *Exodus*.

1952

Jan	First Lancaster B.Mk 1 (modified) delivered to the Aéronavale.

1956

The RAF retires the Lancaster from frontline service.

1963

The RAF retires its final Lincoln.

DESIGN AND DEVELOPMENT

On 10 January 1910, Edwin Alliot Verdon Roe and Humphrey Verdon Roe established a company to build aeroplanes for the enthusiast in Manchester. This was A.V. Roe and Company, commonly known as Avro. Shortly after it formed, a young aircraft designer persuaded Alliot Roe to employ him, and by 1914, at just 21 years old, the young designer was in charge of a workforce of 100.

His name was Roy Chadwick and he was instrumental in the design of the early Avro 500-series aircraft, which included the 504, a machine that became the mainstay of RAF pilot training until the 1930s. Later he was responsible for the creation of the World War II Lancaster and Cold War Vulcan.

In 1914, Roy Dobson joined Avro and by 1918 was works manager, beginning a long working relationship with Chadwick. Dobson was appointed general manager in 1934 and managing director in 1941. Avro was sold to J. D. Siddeley in 1928, and Chadwick appointed chief designer before becoming a company director in 1936. Dobson and Chadwick continued working closely together, Chadwick on aircraft design and Dobson overseeing production – the pieces necessary for the Lancaster's creation were in place.

THE MANCHESTER

The Air Ministry issued a succession of bomber specifications between the wars, but quite deliberately took many of them no further than the prototype stage, preferring to spend its limited budget on maximising the number of bombers in service rather than developing new types. In this way, Britain kept

OPPOSITE Roy Chadwick (right), designer of the Lancaster, discussing the design of the company's new Avro York transport aircraft with draughtsmen in the Drawing Office at an Avro factory in Greater Manchester, March 1942. The York is derived from the Lancaster bomber. (Photo by Saidman/CPL/Paul Popper/Popperfoto/Getty Images)

abreast of technological and aeronautical development through the design and construction of prototypes, while keeping its bomber force at the maximum size affordable, albeit with increasingly obsolete types.

The 1930s saw priority given to the production of twin-engined light/medium bombers, resulting in the Blenheim, Wellington and Hampden being available in quantity when war broke out.

Long-range heavy bomber development had been virtually dormant since the introduction of the Handley Page Heyford. The Fairey Hendon, Handley Page Harrow and Armstrong Whitworth Whitley were classified as heavy bombers, but the Hendon and Harrow carried bomb loads of only 2,600lb and 3,200lb, respectively. The Whitley had a bomb load of 7,000lb, but was a development of the AW.23 bomber transport, with a new low-profile fuselage, and was very much an interim, expedient aircraft.

More ambitious heavy bombers resulted from two Air Ministry Specifications issued during 1936. The first, B.12/36, called for a four-engined 'heavy',

carrying a bomb load of 12,000lb (or 24 troops in the transport role) and a crew of six. It led to orders for two prototypes each of the Supermarine Type 317/318, and for what became the Short Stirling.

Specification P.13/36 outlined a smaller aircraft, still with a six-man crew, powered by twin Rolls-Royce Vulture engines and carrying an 8,000lb bomb load, two aerial torpedoes or 12 troops. A large bomb bay was required to house the offensive weapons, but equipped for interchangeable bomb and fuel configurations for greater operational flexibility.

Introducing new and more specialised roles, its crew comprised two pilots, a navigator, bomb aimer, wireless operator and air gunner. The design requirement also called for a power-operated turret in the nose (two guns) and another in the tail (four guns), a range of not less than 2,000 miles at a speed of not less than 275mph at 15,000ft.

The Air Ministry decided to employ two very high-performance engines in preference to four of the existing motors then available in the 800 to 1,000hp category, and the new Rolls-Royce Vulture was selected. It consisted of two sets of Peregrine V12 cylinder blocks mounted together to use a common crankshaft, resulting in a 24-cylinder engine of 'X' cross-section.

The Vulture gave a high power-to-weight ratio and resulted in a powerplant less costly than four engines. Rolls-Royce began design work in 1935, the engine first was tested in 1937, and by August 1939 the Vulture II was producing a promising 1,800hp. It was not perfect, however, suffering connecting rod failures that required a reduction in engine speed, yet it still produced encouraging results. In service the engine developed a habit of catching fire in flight, an issue that plagued it throughout its service; other problems also emerged, resulting in deplorable reliability.

OPPOSITE Wellington Bombers in formation, 1940. The Vickers Wellington was a British twin-engined, long range medium bomber, widely used as a night bomber in the early years of World War II. (Photo by Print Collector/Getty Images)

A number of companies entered bids for P.13/36. The Bristol Aeroplane Company submitted a design for a shoulder wing monoplane capable of achieving 315mph, but it used a pair of Bristol Hercules radial engines. The design was rejected, as was a Hawker design for a mid-wing monoplane using two Vultures.

Handley Page submitted the H.P.56, intended for a pair of Vultures but subsequently redesigned for four Rolls-Royce Merlin engines once concerns over the viability of the Vulture arose. The design became the H.P.57, later named Halifax.

The last design standing was Avro's, the Type 679, first submitted in September 1936. It was for a twin-Vulture layout with a 69ft-long fuselage coupled to a 72ft wing that tapered in planform and thickness towards the tips, and with a tail unit comprising twin fins and rudders.

The front crew was accommodated forward of the main spar, where positions were provided for two pilots, a navigator/bomb aimer and a wireless operator/front gunner. The remaining two crew were both air gunners and positioned aft of the main spar in ventral and tail turrets. The specification called for Chadwick's team to build an airframe the like of which they had not produced before, requiring a novel configuration, with stressed skinning and of a weight and power not yet attempted. In September 1936 the Air Ministry invited Avro to build two prototypes, with the aircraft to be called the Manchester.

FROM HUMBLE BEGINNINGS

The first prototype Manchester, L7246, was built at Avro's Newton Heath factory, the main sections being transported to Ringway airfield for assembly during May 1939. It was not fitted with turrets, and their locations were faired over for flight test. The Manchester first flew on 25 July 1939, with Avro's chief test pilot Captain H. A. 'Sam' Brown at the controls.

The aircraft exhibited several handling faults, including an issue with lateral stability and other problems caused by high wing loading. The Aeroplane & Armament Experimental Establishment (A&AEE)

at Boscombe Down made similar observations when it received L7246 for RAF evaluation. The tests also revealed that the Vulture Mk I engines were limited in boost and lacked power.

Despite these teething troubles the design was generally praised, however, particularly with reference to its speed and altitude performance. The Manchester was viewed as a major step forward in bomber design regardless of the issues with its powerplant, which, it was hoped, would be resolved by the improved engines intended for the second prototype.

Shortcomings aside, events in Europe and the immediate threat of war resulted in plans for mass production of the Manchester being put in place before either prototype had flown. It was to be produced in Avro's plants at Newton Heath and Woodford, Manchester, as well as the Metropolitan-Vickers plant at Trafford Park, Manchester, from 1938.

The second prototype, L7247, differed from its predecessor in having a redesigned and extended outer wing and new fins and rudder. It flew for the first time on 26 May 1940 and while generally successful, the lateral stability problem remained. The airframe was modified almost immediately, with the addition of a third fin on the upper centreline of the rear fuselage to resolve the issue.

Further modifications were made throughout 1940, including the installation of improved Vulture II engines, a larger central fin and hydraulically actuated Frazer Nash turrets in the nose, tail and ventral positions. The ventral turret became a cause for concern, however, since when lowered it produced sufficient drag to slow the aircraft by 15kt. The 'dustbin', as it became known, was also heavy and crudely designed.

Production contracts were awarded for 1,200 Manchesters. Newton Heath took the first orders under Contract B.648770/37, for an initial run of 200 airframes, and Metropolitan-Vickers at Trafford Park was tasked to build 100 under Contract B.108750/40, a requirement later expanded to include a further 300 airframes built by the Fairey Aviation Company and

Sir W. G. Armstrong Whitworth and Co. The first production aircraft, L7276, was delivered to the A&AEE on 5 August 1940.

A CURATE'S EGG

After the summer of 1940 and the exploits of 'The Few' in the Battle of Britain, it appeared that Britain was safe from invasion for the time being. Thoughts at RAF High Command swung from defence to attack and the new Manchester seemed to offer the opportunity not only to take the war to Germany, but right into its heartland, which the shorter-ranged medium bombers struggled to reach.

The RAF and Avro believed there was insufficient time to develop the new aircraft further and that it should enter service as soon as possible. The urgent need to strike back at Germany was coupled with trial results suggesting the aircraft's issues would be

overcome. The Manchester was rushed into service with new Vulture Mk II engines which, while a definite improvement on the original, still lacked power and were prone to overheating and catching fire.

The first Manchesters were issued to No. 207 Squadron, which had reformed at RAF Waddington on 1 November 1940 under Squadron Leader Noel Hyde. The unit was responsible for bringing the new aircraft up to operational standard by developing crew training regimes and new tactics; it took L7279, its first Manchester, on 6 November. Over the next six weeks the squadron's strength reached 11 aircraft and 16 crews, including some of Bomber Command's most experienced airmen.

Technical faults with the Vulture and airframe issues delayed the aircraft's entry into operational service, but these were overcome and the Manchester undertook its first missions on the night of 24 February 1941. Six aircraft took part in a raid on Brest, where the German cruiser *Admiral Hipper* had been reported. Despite the Manchesters performing as expected, the ship was not

OPPOSITE Armstrong Whitworth Whitley B.Mk I K7191. (Cody Images)

damaged. The aircraft had taken part in operations just 18 months after the prototype had first flown.

Despite this initial 'success', the first squadron aircraft were early Mk I airframes with the original triple fin arrangement. They lacked dorsal turrets and were unable to carry the 2,000lb bomb that had been one of the design advantages of the aircraft over its competitors. Within a month of commencing operations, however, No. 207 Sqn began receiving updated airframes with several improvements, including the addition of a Frazer Nash FN7 dorsal turret mounting two 0.303in Browning machine guns.

But the arrival of this improved Mk I did not resolve the engine issues. Number 207 Sqn suffered its first loss on the night of 20 March when L7278 crashed following an engine fire on take-off, killing both pilots and two other crew.

ABOVE Avro Manchester Mk I L7571/EM-S served No. 207 Sqn, the first unit to receive the type. Note the Vulture engines and the tail assembly following removal of the central fin. (Cody Images)

Despite its shortcomings, a second squadron was formed and equipped with the Manchester the day after 207's first operational sortie. Number 97 Sqn was established at Waddington under Squadron Leader Denys Balsdon and undertook its first operation on the night of 8 April, when four of its Manchesters took part in a raid against Kiel. All returned safely, but on the same night a 207 Sqn Manchester commanded by Noel Hyde failed to return. The loss of Hyde's aircraft was considered a major setback to the Manchester's early operational career, since he had been instrumental in bringing the aircraft to operational readiness.

GROUNDED

By April 1941 sufficient operational hours had been flown to enable detailed analysis of the Vulture's capabilities and weaknesses. Close examination of stripped-down engines revealed that the X arrangement of cylinders caused the overheating problem, restricting cooling and affecting the lubrication of the big-end bearings. On 13 April 1941 all Manchesters were grounded until a solution to the problem could be found.

While the aircraft were grounded, Avro engineers took the opportunity to make changes bringing them closer to the design specification. Among these were the general adoption of the dorsal turret and changes to the bomb bay enabling the aircraft to carry a 4,000lb 'Cookie' bomb.

The Manchester was released back into service following engine modifications and on the night of 2 May it resumed operations. One of 207 Sqn's aircraft was the first Manchester to drop the new 'Cookie' on a target, although Wellington crews had already used the weapon. The Manchester soldiered on and by the end of May 1941 had flown 100 operational sorties.

It is difficult to assess the aircraft's effectiveness during its first three months of service.

Even so, it is clear that the unreliable Vulture was the reason for many aborted sorties, which affected as many as one in five aircraft. It also appears that more Manchesters were lost as a result of technical failure than as a result of enemy action. Engine issues grounded the Manchester again on 16 June, the type returning to service six days later. A week after that it was grounded again, for 'engine overhauls'.

Engine unreliability continued, however, and unserviceability had become so serious by July 1941 that the Manchester squadrons were forced to make use of obsolete Hampdens to make up the numbers required for operations. Doubts were beginning to be expressed about the Manchester's future, but after much discussion in the RAF's higher echelons it was decided to persevere with the aircraft in a modified form. The central fin was to be removed and the size of the tailplanes and remaining fins increased in size to improve lateral stability. The improved Manchester was designated Mk IA.

While the changes were being made, another Manchester unit was established, No. 61 Sqn, which

OPPOSITE The forward section of an Avro Manchester Mk I of No. 207 Sqn RAF, while running up the port Rolls-Royce Vulture II engine at Waddington, Lincolnshire, showing the nose with the bomb-aimer's window, the forward gun-turret and the pilot's cockpit, 12 September 1941. (Photo by B. J. Daventry/ IWM via Getty Images)

formed at North Luffenham on 17 July. Manchester operations recommenced on the night of 7 August and throughout the remainder of 1941 the Manchester units continued working up new crews, gradually increasing the number of operational sorties. A fourth unit, No. 83 Sqn, began re-equipping at Scampton in December 1941, commencing operations in January 1942.

But the Manchester's contribution to Bomber Command's efforts remained small. Its introduction to service was frustratingly slow, leaving the main workload to other types. Even though the aircraft had been in service for ten months, the number of operational machines and crews was extremely small, and by the end of 1941 there were only four operational Manchester squadrons (7 per cent of Bomber Command's total strength) as opposed to 21 operational Wellington squadrons. On 7 September 1941, Bomber Command sent 198 aircraft to Berlin, only four of which were Manchesters, and on 7 November its entire serviceable strength was sent to Berlin, including only 15 Manchesters.

Despite its now obvious failure, the RAF was forced to persevere with the type in late 1941 since there was no alternative. The Stirling was beginning to look doubtful and the Halifax remained unproven with only a handful of units. The only other option was to re-equip the Manchester units with Wellingtons and obsolete Hampdens, but this would have been a backward step. Something dramatic needed to be done to solve the Manchester's failings.

LEFT Designed in 1932, the Rolls-Royce Merlin was the most important aero engine of World War II. It powered the Spitfire and the Hurricane fighters during the Battle of Britain in 1940 as well as the Lancaster and Mosquito. When the Merlin first entered service it produced 750 horse power, which was more than doubled over the period of the war, reaching well over 2000 horse power. (Photo by SSPL/Getty Images)

FOUR ENGINES

Meanwhile, Avro had considered replacing the Vultures with either Bristol Centaurus radial engines or Napier Sabre I inlines. A Manchester airframe was sent to Napier at Luton for Sabres to be installed, but as it became clear that the Sabre would require lengthy development, it was discarded as an option for the bomber. Two Centaurus engines were fitted to another Manchester test airframe, which was then designated Manchester Mk II. The Centaurus was a more powerful development of the Hercules fitted to the Stirling, but despite the promise the engine and airframe combination appeared to offer, the Manchester II never flew, being superseded by the extremely promising Mk III.

Roy Chadwick had been considering the possibility of adapting the Manchester to accommodate four engines since before the war, as soon as it became obvious that the Vulture was going to leave the type underpowered. He also thought that the four-engined Stirling and Halifax would offer increased range and improved bomb load, as well as greater potential for future development. The Manchester still represented a basically a good design, with one distinct advantage over the Stirling and Halifax – it had been designed with a large bomb bay.

Various options were discussed for a four-engined Manchester III. The Bristol Taurus and Pegasus engines were discarded fairly quickly, since Chadwick believed the most sensible choice was the proven Merlin (as fitted to the early Halifax) or Hercules.

Fitting two additional engines increased the aircraft's weight by 12.5 per cent over the Manchester I for the Merlin option, and added a further 1,000lb for the Hercules. In response, Chadwick and his design team considered strengthening the undercarriage and changing the tail assembly.

The four-engined Manchester proposal was designated Avro Type 680, but not considered a serious competitor to the other two four-engined bombers in development, until the Air Ministry issued specification B.1/39 on 6 March 1939. It called for a four-engined bomber with a maximum all-up weight of 50,000lb, including a bomb load of 1,000lb and two cannon-armed turrets. The new

OPPOSITE A Lancaster from the historic Battle of Britain Memorial Flight performs a fly-past during an air show. (Stuart Gray/Getty Images)

aircraft was to have a crew of seven and be capable of an operating range of more than 2,500 miles at a cruising speed of 250mph at 15,000ft.

Sholto Douglas, the Assistant Chief of Air Staff (ACAS), insisted the project be progressed as a matter of urgency and several designs were considered. They included the Armstrong Whitworth A.W.58, which suffered from cramped crew accommodation; Bristol 159, which had issues due to its two-tier bomb stowage; Handley Page H.P.60, again with poor crew accommodation; Shorts S.34 and Vickers 405, both disliked owing to issues with their defensive armament; and the Avro 680. The Air Ministry believed that the Handley Page and Bristol proposals had the most promise and four full-scale prototypes were ordered in late December 1939. The Avro Type 680 was not to be proceeded with.

However, events transpired to bring the Avro offering back to the table. In May 1940 Air Vice Marshal Tedder wrote that the four prototypes for the B.1/39 'Ideal Bomber' project should be suspended amid concerns about proceeding with such an advanced aircraft, and in July Handley Page and Bristol were informed that design work should cease. The German advance into France convinced the Ministry of Aircraft Production that work should concentrate on certain types of aircraft, and the 'Ideal Bomber' was retired to obscurity.

The RAF then removed the restriction that had plagued the earlier bomber designs, which dictated that all new bombers must be able to operate from existing RAF airfields. This opened the doors for Chadwick to design an aircraft with a longer and thinner wing of stronger construction and capable of taking four engines. The result was the Avro Type 683, powered by four Merlin X engines and with increased wingspan over the Manchester Mk I, and an enlarged tailplane.

The outbreak of war in 1939 resulted in Avro concentrating on bringing the Manchester into service, but the four-engined Manchester remained under development at Avro under Stuart Davies. The Type 683 project revealed that the aircraft would exceed the performance laid down in the specification, with improved operating speed, altitude and bomb capacity.

Avro had always believed that a four-engined bomber would eventually replace the Manchester, but the thought that this might be the Halifax or Stirling was unwelcome. Avro's designers believed the more sensible option was for the Manchester to be replaced by a four-engined variant to ensure commonality of parts and training. Once the Manchester I had entered service, Avro gave greater importance to the Type 683, although the project almost stalled once again.

The Manchester's issues had convinced the Ministry of Aircraft Production that Avro's facilities should be turned over to Halifax production. Within hours of receiving notification that this might be the case, Chadwick and Dobson went to the Ministry with full performance estimates for the Type 683 and won an order for two prototypes to be produced by July 1941.

In fact a contract was awarded for four prototypes of a four-engined bomber to replace the Manchester. The first was to feature a modified Manchester fuselage and Merlin X engines, the second to be representative of the final production airframe and the third to be fitted with Hercules engines. The fourth was never built. Chadwick and Dobson had earned a reprieve and the Manchester Mk III became a reality.

THE MAKING OF A LEGEND

Avro received authority to go ahead with the four prototype Manchester III airframes on 19 November 1940. To save time, Manchester Mk I BT308 was taken off the production line and fitted with four 12-cylinder, 60° upright-vee, liquid-cooled Merlin X inline engines with single-stage centrifugal superchargers, to become the first prototype Manchester III. Avro experienced difficulty in getting engines due to the Ministry of Aircraft Production's determination that all Merlins should be reserved for desperately needed Spitfire and Hurricane production, but Chadwick and Dobson acquired four engines for BT308 from a close friend at Rolls-Royce. Yet another obstacle in their path had been overcome.

Chadwick and Davies then agreed that BT308 should retain the standard Manchester fuselage assembly but that its wings would be modified with new outer panels and powerplant assemblies. The aircraft would retain the standard Manchester undercarriage and electrical system, powered by the inner engines, along with a larger, 33ft tailplane mounting standard Manchester fins. BT308 would also retain the centreline fin.

The inner engines were located at the same points on the wing as the Manchester's Vultures. The outer engines were fitted as far inboard as permitted by the diameter of their propeller arcs.

The cockpit was similar to that of production Manchester Mk Is, but with a wider centre console to accommodate four throttle levers side by side, with propeller controls mounted underneath, rather than alongside the throttles as they were on the Mk I. The flight instruments remained as for the Mk I, other than the addition of gauges for the additional engines.

BT308 was completed and transported to Ringway (now Manchester International Airport) for its first flight, which was delayed by changes to the hydraulic system and fog. It finally took place on 9 January 1941 with Avro test pilots 'Sam' Brown and Bill Thorn at the controls. It was successful, and nine more test flights followed in quick succession before BT308 was handed over to the A&AEE at Boscombe Down on 27 February for intensive flight trials.

Meanwhile, Avro had determined that the bomber needed a new name. The designers had informally christened the project 'Lancaster' and used the name for some time when referring to the Type 683, although it had not been recognised by the Air Ministry. On 28 February 1941 the name was formally approved, however, and the aircraft officially christened.

OPPOSITE Lancaster B.Mk I R5689/VN-N of No. 50 Sqn shows the faired-in mid-upper turret and unpainted fuselage windows. The pilot has the sliding cockpit window open. (Cody Images)

A NEW BOMBER FOR THE RAF

After A&AEE trials, BT308 returned to Avro for

installation of a new tail section, with the central fin deleted. Boscombe Down's trials had proven successful, with only slight directional stability issues reported, and the new tail assembly was expected to solve these. The modified BT308 returned to Boscombe Down for preliminary service evaluation and in September 1941 it was delivered to RAF Waddington for familiarisation and crew training.

Meanwhile the second prototype, DG595, made its maiden flight of 20 minutes on 13 May 1941. It was built as close as possible to production standard, stressed to the maximum production weight of 60,000lb all-up and capable of carrying a full warload, including FN50 dorsal and FN64 ventral gun turrets. Power came from the Merlin XX.

The third prototype, DT810, made its first flight on 26 November 1941, by which time the first production Lancaster Mk I had already flown. DT810 was, according to the initial order, to be the prototype Lancaster Mk II, powered by four air-cooled, two-row, 14-cylinder Hercules VI sleeve-valve radial engines with two-speed centrifugal superchargers. The fourth prototype, DT812, was not built.

In anticipation of the Lancaster being successful, the original production order for 1,200 Manchesters was amended. The contract awarded to Avro at Newton Heath was altered so that the first 157 aircraft would be completed as Manchester Mk I/IA airframes, the remaining 43 as Lancasters. The contract awarded to Metropolitan-Vickers for 100 Manchesters required the first 43 to be completed as Manchester Mk I/IA and the remaining 57 as Lancasters. The initial orders for Fairey and Armstrong Whitworth for 300 Manchesters were cancelled.

In order to co-ordinate Lancaster production across different factories, the Lancaster Production Group was set up in September 1941. It originally comprised Avro's Newton Heath and new, Chadderton, factories, Metropolitan-Vickers at Trafford Park and Armstrong

ABOVE A Lancaster B.Mk III, showing the standard Bomber Command camouflage pattern used up until the end of the war. (Cody Images)

Whitworth in Coventry; Vickers-Armstrong at Castle Bromwich joined later. Increased demand for Lancasters resulted in further expansion, the group subsequently including Vickers at Chester and the Austin Motor Company (Austin Aero) in Birmingham.

The first production Lancaster, L7527, joined the production line as a Manchester I, but was modified to Lancaster Mk I standard. It flew for the first time from Woodford on 31 October 1941, and several suggestions for modifications were made. The most significant was removal of the ventral turret, which was considered to be of little use, especially in night operations.

The A&AEE at Boscombe Down declared the aircraft fit for service with Bomber Command. It had been decided to re-equip one of the squadrons operating the obsolete Hampden first as part of the phasing out of that aircraft, rather than a Manchester squadron. The first three airframes were therefore delivered to No. 44 (Rhodesia) Squadron at Waddington, on 24 December 1941, with four more arriving four days later to begin replacement of its Hampdens. The decision meant that the Lancaster would serve for a short time alongside its less illustrious forebear.

New production orders were awarded to the Lancaster Production Group. Contract B.69274/40 went to Avro at Newton Heath for a total of 650 Lancaster Mk I aircraft. The figure was later revised to 407, to be delivered in two batches. The first batch of 200 was for delivery between February and July 1942, the second batch of 207 between July and November 1942. Contract B.69275/40 was awarded to Metropolitan-Vickers for 170 Mk I and 30 Mk III aircraft to be delivered between September 1942 and May 1943.

TECHNICAL SPECIFICATIONS

The Lancaster was designed for a crew of seven, initially including a second pilot, but the role was removed early in the type's gestation when a pilot shortage made the provision a luxury the force could not afford. Instead, another crewmember was trained as the pilot's assistant.

Meanwhile, the increasing specialisation of navigation and bomb aiming resulted in the two tasks becoming separate, provision for which had also been made in the Lancaster's design. Another role was flight engineer, a position resulting from the complexity of the modern four-engined bombers. The standard Lancaster crew therefore comprised the pilot, who also commanded the aircraft, navigator, flight engineer, bomb aimer (who doubled as front gunner when not engaged in his bomb-aiming role), wireless operator, mid-upper gunner and tail gunner.

The Lancaster airframe was of all-metal construction, 59ft 6in long, with a wingspan of 102ft and 20ft in height. The fuselage was built as a light alloy monocoque. It accommodated the crew and their equipment, the bomb bay and defensive armament. Roughly oval in cross section, it was broken down for production into five modular units: the nose section, front fuselage, intermediate section, rear centre and rear fuselage. Each was fully assembled and equipped before they were brought together.

The nose section included a hemispherical transparent perspex dome, usually incorporating a flat,

OPPOSITE RAF fitters work on a Lancaster's Merlin engines. (Cody Images)

circular glass vision panel for bomb aiming. The forward escape hatch was built into the floor and the walls had numerous windows for the bomb aimer. The forward power-operated FN5 turret was fitted above and behind the bomb aimer's blister.

The forward fuselage section contained the main cockpit area, including the pilot's position on a raised platform on the forward port side. The cockpit and cabin area also housed the navigator, wireless operator and flight engineer. The forward part of the bomb bay was below the cabin floor. Combined, the nose and forward fuselage sections were just over 20ft in length and remained joined for transport.

The intermediate centre section was 8ft long and constructed around the front and rear main spars. The centre section roof contained an emergency escape hatch, while the bomb bay continued under its floor.

The rear centre section was more than 20ft in length, extending from the trailing edge of the wing to the tail. It included the power-operated FN50 dorsal turret and, on early aircraft, an FN64 ventral turret aft

of the bomb bay. A small emergency escape hatch was located in the rear centre section's roof. Its floor formed a walkway to the rear of the aircraft, with the aft bomb bay area below. The 33ft-long bay extended across the forward fuselage, intermediate and rear centre sections.

The rear fuselage section was 21ft long and built around the tailplane spars, which passed through aft; the tailwheel assembly was mounted below. The rear section contained the main crew door, to starboard, and a power-operated FN20 turret at its extreme rear. The tail unit comprised a 33ft-span tailplane, mounting 12ft-tall endplate fins and rudders.

The Lancaster's dihedralled cantilever wings were built around the forward and aft main spars in the fuselage centre section. For construction and transportation they were divided into sub-assemblies: the centre section, two outer wing sections (port and starboard) and two wing tip sections (port and starboard).

The wing centre section spanned 25ft and was integral with the fuselage centre section. The inboard engine nacelles were located on the wing centre section. They housed the main undercarriage, which retracted backwards into the extended nacelle aft section.

The outer wing and wing tip sections had a combined span of 74ft. The outer engine nacelles were fitted to the outer wing sections, which mounted ailerons at their trailing edges. The wings carried hydraulically actuated split flaps and four fuel tanks, later increased to six. Fully assembled, the wings had an area of 1,300sqft.

The main undercarriage comprised a retractable Dowty oleo-pneumatic system, each unit equipped with a single wheel and tyre. A safety bolt locked the cockpit undercarriage lever down to prevent accidental retraction on the ground; it had to be moved aside for the undercarriage to be retracted in flight. Undercarriage indicators in the cockpit showed two

OPPOSITE A mechanic works on the nose of an Avro Lancaster bomber, 16 April 1943. (Photo by Keystone Features/Getty Images)

green lights when the gear was locked down and two red lights when it was locked up. The Lancaster Mk X differed in having a pictorial undercarriage indicator. A warning horn sounded if either inboard throttle was closed when the undercarriage was not locked down. The tailwheel was a non-retracting Dowty oleo-pneumatic assembly.

THE LANCASTER: MARK BY MARK

Identifying Lancaster variants, or marks, can be tricky since external variations were often subtle.

LANCASTER B.MK I

The first squadron to receive the Lancaster Mk I was No. 44 (Rhodesia) Squadron. Typically for a new aircraft, the Lancaster suffered teething troubles; R5539 crashed during a dive test after tailplane skin failure, for example. Other minor issues led to the wing tips being strengthened and the fuel system was modified to prevent airlocks causing fuel pump blockages. The basic durability of the design meant these teething troubles did not affect operational availability, however, and most modifications were made for operational reasons.

The ventral turret was quickly deleted from production airframes due to the perception that it was of little use. Its employment was hampered by poor visibility and the lack of a dedicated crewmember to operate it. The Mk I therefore saw service with and without it.

The mid-upper turret on early production aircraft was unfaired, leaving the gunner with unrestricted depression of his weapons and in a danger of firing on his own aircraft. In late 1942 a contoured fairing was added around the turret. It incorporated a track in which wheeled stalks ran that were connected to the guns, ensuring the weapons could not train on any part of the aircraft. Thus, in-service Mk I airframes also featured a mix of faired and unfaired turrets.

The fuselage retained rows of small rectangular windows inherited from the Manchester, but these were often painted over, giving the impression that they did not exist. The forward pair of windows in the

LANCASTER B.MK I SPECIFICATION

Powerplant: 4 × 1,280hp Rolls-Royce Merlin XX engines driving clockwise-rotating three-bladed de Havilland DH.5/40 variable-pitch airscrews, interchangeable with Hamilton Standard A 5/138 airscrews

Length: 59ft 6in (18.1m)

Height: 20ft (6.1m)

Wingspan: 102ft (31.1m)

Wing area: 1,300sqft (120.8m²)

Weight (empty): 37,000lb (16,783kg)

Weight (normal take-off): 65,000lb (29,484kg)

Maximum speed at 15,000ft: 275mph (443km/h)

Range (with 7,000lb load): 2,530 miles (4,070km)

Range (with 12,000lb load): 1,700 miles (2,736km)

Service ceiling: 24,500ft

Defensive armament (early aircraft): 2 × Browning 0.303in (7.7mm) machine guns each in power-operated FN5 nose and FN50 mid-upper turrets; 1 × Browning 0.303in machine gun in power-operated FN64 ventral turret; 4 × Browning 0.303in machine guns in power-operated FN20 tail turret

Defensive armament (later aircraft): 2 × Browning 0.303in machine guns each in power-operated FN5 nose and FN50 mid-upper turrets; 4 × Browning 0.303in machine guns in power-operated FN20 tail turret

Offensive armament: Up to 14,000lb (6,350kg) of bombs and other freefall ordnance

fuselage side was deleted from the JB/LM production series on.

Some production aircraft were fitted with an enlarged bomb aimer's blister, which featured a shallower-angled, optically flat aiming panel. In addition, during 1942, bulged bomb bay doors appeared on selected aircraft to accommodate the new 8,000lb bomb.

The original turrets on Mk I aircraft were badly affected by rain and dirt, and a sliding panel was fitted

LANCASTER B.MK II SPECIFICATION

(Data as Mk I unless specified)

Powerplant: 4 × 1,735hp Bristol Hercules XVI engines driving counter-clockwise rotating three-bladed Rotol variable-pitch airscrews (aircraft DS601-DS627 had 1,735hp Hercules VI engines)

Weight (normal take-off): 63,000lb (28,576kg)

Maximum speed at 14,000ft: 265mph (426km/h)

Range at 15,000ft: 2,370 miles (3,814km)

Service ceiling: 18,500ft

Defensive armament: 2 × Browning 0.303in machine guns each in power-operated FN5A nose, FN50 mid-upper and FN64 ventral turrets; 4 × Browning 0.303in machine guns in FN20 or FN120 power-operated tail turret (some late aircraft were fitted with a single 0.5in/12.7mm Browning machine gun in the fuselage floor in place of the FN64 turret in early 1944)

to some tail turrets. Later, the entire central perspex panel was removed on some aircraft, giving much improved visibility for only a marginal temperature drop for the gunner, who worked in an already cold environment.

The leading edges of early aircraft were smeared with de-icing paste, but later airframes had thermal de-icing equipment as standard.

LANCASTER B.MK II

The Lancaster Mk II was a result of concerns that demand placed upon Rolls-Royce for the Merlin engine might produce a bottleneck in airframe production; the Merlin powered the Spitfire, Hurricane, Whitley, Wellington, Battle, Beaufighter and other types.

There was also concern about the vulnerability that came with having one engine type satisfy so many power requirements, should the Luftwaffe disrupt Merlin production. This fear, despite ongoing discussions for US Merlin production, resulted in the need to find an alternative Lancaster powerplant. Indeed, the concept of the four-engined Manchester had barely been proven when the Air Ministry officially acknowledged the need for an alternative and the

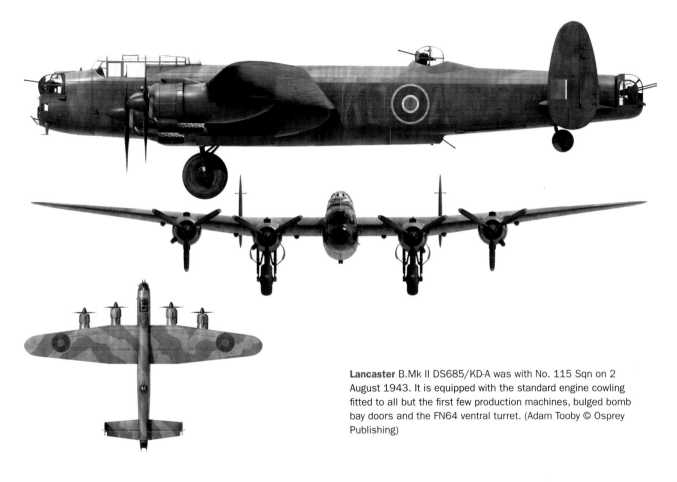

Lancaster B.Mk II DS685/KD-A was with No. 115 Sqn on 2 August 1943. It is equipped with the standard engine cowling fitted to all but the first few production machines, bulged bomb bay doors and the FN64 ventral turret. (Adam Tooby © Osprey Publishing)

Hercules was selected.

The Air Ministry placed an order for two Mk II prototypes (DT810 and DT812) and a healthy production order almost immediately. In the event, only DT810 was built as a prototype, and sent to the A&AEE at Boscombe Down for testing before series production began. Avro and Metropolitan-Vickers were heavily engaged in Lancaster B.Mk I production and neither could accept a contract for the Mk II. Nonetheless, Avro's experimental department produced the prototype in very short order, since a supply of components was readily available at the Chadderton plant, enabling its engineers to hand build DT810 and overcome any issues in fitting the Hercules.

Production was contracted to Armstrong Whitworth's Newton Road, Nuneaton works, but it was heavily engaged with Whitley production, which had unexpectedly been extended in 1941 when RAF Coastal Command placed orders for the radar-equipped Whitley Mk VII, and the Lancaster Mk II order was therefore delayed until May 1941.

The Ministry of Aircraft Production finally ordered a halt to Whitley production in March 1942 so that Lancaster Mk II production could begin under order 239/SAS/C4(C) for 200 aircraft, with delivery required between September 1942 and October 1943. The order was later extended to include another 100 aircraft, for delivery between October 1943 and March 1944. It took a full 12 months for the switch from Whitley to Lancaster, Armstrong Whitworth systematically replacing production jigs and tools as the last Whitleys moved down the line.

The first Mk IIs, DS601 and DS602, were delivered to Boscombe Down for service trials. The aircraft was pronounced virtually faultless, but although the Hercules engines were more powerful than the early Merlins, offsetting their increased drag over the sleek Merlin installation, they required greater care in management and used more fuel; this issue was remedied in later Mk IIs, which employed the improved Hercules XVI. The first Lancaster Mk II unit was No. 61 Sqn at RAF Syerston.

The Bristol radial changed the aircraft's lines considerably. The first few production machines were fitted with the Hercules VI, but the Hercules XVI soon became standard. Both engines were rated at 1,735hp and the only practical method for identifying which type was fitted is by reference to serial numbers.

The Mk II was initially identical to the Mk I other than in its engine fit, but gained extended bomb doors as standard early in the production run, so that it could accommodate the 8,000lb bomb. The FN64 ventral turret was re-introduced after Bomber Command encountered German night fighters equipped with upward-firing *Schräge Musik* cannon.

The lighter Frazer-Nash FN120 turret featured improved gun sights and often replaced the FN20 in the Mk II's tail position. The model was also fitted with the shallow nose blister.

Other refinements included the installation of bell-shaped spinners on the propeller hubs and Beaufighter-pattern air intakes, identified by the shorter intake feed pipe that begins just forward of the cooling gills on the cowling, where the early fit extends to just aft of the cowling ring. Later production Mk IIs also had flame-damping exhausts.

The fears over Merlin engine supply never materialised, the Halifax Mk III was made the priority for Hercules production and there were no further Lancaster Mk II orders. Armstrong Whitworth thus completed 300 Mk IIs before switching to the Lancaster B.Mk I/III.

LANCASTER B.MK III

Licensed production of Packard Merlins began relatively quickly, since Rolls-Royce had anticipated the need to source engines from the US, where production was less likely to be disrupted by enemy action.

The first prototype Lancaster B.Mk III, W4114, fitted with Packard Merlin 28 engines, was delivered to the A&AEE for trials in October 1942. Contract B.69274/40 was awarded to Avro for a fourth production batch of 620 Lancaster Mk I/IIIs for delivery between November 1942 and June 1943.

Contract B.69275/40, awarded to Metropolitan-Vickers, was amended to include a further 200 Mk Is and IIIs for delivery between May and November 1943. A new contract (No. 1807), the largest for Lancasters, was also awarded to Avro. It ordered 900 Mk Is and IIIs for construction at Newton Heath and delivery commencing June 1943, after completion of existing Lancaster production contracts, with a further 350 to be built at Avro's new Yeadon plant, for delivery commencing November 1942.

Lancaster production used Rolls-Royce and Packard Merlins as quickly as they were available. When the Packard Merlin was fitted to an aircraft on the production line it was designated as a Mk III. When Rolls-Royce engines were installed, the aircraft was a Mk I. The only external difference between the variants was serial number, although this only indicated what mark the aircraft was built to, not what it may have become in service.

As flying hours mounted, engines were often changed because of failures or battle damage, or

LANCASTER B.MK III SPECIFICATION

(*Data as Mk I unless specified*)

Powerplant: 4 × 1,420hp Packard Merlin 28 engines

Defensive armament: 2 × Browning 0.303in machine guns each in power-operated FN5 nose and FN50 mid-upper turrets; 4 × Browning 0.303in machine guns in power-operated FN20 tail turret

because it was demanded by the RAF's maintenance schedule. Since the Packard and Rolls-Royce Merlins were interchangeable, maintenance units used replacement engines available from new deliveries or reconditioned stock, regardless of origins. Thus a

OPPOSITE Women's Auxiliary Air Force fitter works on the equipment in a Lancaster bomb aimer's position. The gangway into the nose section was fitted with handrails to assist the crewman. The panel directly above the WAAF is the rear of the front turret fairing; when the turret was manned the gunner's legs would dangle into the space occupied by the WAAF, the turret having no floor. (Cody Images)

Lancaster Mk I could be fitted with replacement Packard engines, becoming a 'Mk III', or vice versa; it was also not uncommon for an aircraft to have a mix of Packard and Rolls-Royce engines. It is therefore best to view the two marks as Lancaster Mk I/III, since it is impossible to determine engine fit without detailed reference to individual aircraft maintenance records.

The Packard had only one important variation compared to the Rolls-Royce engine and that was a tendency to overheat on take-off or landing. While not a particular problem for an experienced pilot to manage, it could prove fatal for a new pilot or one unfamiliar with the Lancaster. Operational training units therefore used only Mk I aircraft.

TYPE 464 'PROVISIONING' LANCASTER

The Type 464 'Provisioning' Lancaster was a modification of the B.Mk I/III airframe to carry Barnes Wallis's Upkeep mine, otherwise known as the 'bouncing bomb', for Operation *Chastise*.

Upkeep required a launch mechanism to induce the backspin required to make it bounce over water. This was fitted in the bomb bay, but its height required that the bomb doors be removed. A hydraulic motor in the middle section of the cabin imparted backspin through a rotating mechanism in the mine's cradle. The launch mechanism's weight was offset by removal of the dorsal turret.

To function correctly, Upkeep required the aircraft to maintain a constant 200mph at 60ft above the water surface. The standard Lancaster altimeter lacked accuracy at such a low altitude and was therefore replaced by a more sensitive radio altimeter.

It was also necessary to find a method for maintaining constant height during the bomb run, and the aircraft was fitted with Aldis lamps, one at the nose and a second aft of the bomb bay, arranged to converge on the ground when the aircraft was precisely 60ft above.

The standard bombsight was replaced with a special sight constructed from a wooden triangle with a wooden peg at each corner of its base. When the pegs lined up with the towers on the dams, the aircraft was

TYPE 464 'PROVISIONING' LANCASTER SPECIFICATION

(Data as Mk I/III unless specified)

Weight (empty): 38,000lb (17,237kg)

Weight (normal take-off): 66,000lb (29,937kg)

Defensive armament: 2 × Browning 0.303in machine guns in power-operated FN5 nose turret; 4 × Browning 0.303in machine guns in power-operated FN20 tail turret

Offensive armament: 1 × 9,250lb Upkeep mine

at the correct distance from the dam wall and the bomb could be released.

Each of the Type 464 Lancasters was allocated a 'G' suffix to its serial number. This indicated that the aircraft was to be guarded on the ground at all times. After the Dams raid, the surviving aircraft were demodified to standard Mk I/III configuration and reissued to squadrons.

LANCASTER B.MK X

By 1942, Canada was already providing a major contribution to the Allied air war with aircrew training facilities far away from Luftwaffe attentions, but the Canadian government wished to contribute further by producing aircraft. Government-owned Victory Aircraft Corporation was therefore created to produce Lancasters under licence.

The aircraft were classified as the Lancaster B. Mk X, and the first 75 fitted with Packard Merlin 38 engines; the remainder employed the Packard Merlin 228. The Mk X was outwardly identical to the B.Mk III, but had enlarged bomb bay doors as standard and reintroduced the FN64 ventral turret. From KB774 onwards, paddle-bladed propellers superseded its original narrow-chord units for improved climb rate and altitude performance.

The majority of the Victory aircraft were flown or shipped across the Atlantic to Britain, where they were issued to Royal Canadian Air Force (RCAF) bomber squadrons operating from the UK.

LANCASTER B.MK X SPECIFICATION

(Data as Mk I/III unless specified)

Powerplant: 4 × Packard Merlin 38 (KB700-KB 774), or 4 × Packard Merlin 228 engines

Weight (normal take-off): 61,500lb (27,896kg)

Defensive armament: 2 × Browning 0.303in machine guns each in power-operated FN5 nose, FN50 mid-upper and FN64 ventral turrets; 4 × Browning 0.303in machine guns in power-operated FN20 tail turret. In later aircraft a Martin turret with 2 × 0.5in Browning machine guns replaced the FN50 mid-upper turret.

LANCASTER B.MK I SPECIAL

The Mk I Special arose from a need to carry another of Barnes Wallis's 'wonder weapons', the 22,000lb

OPPOSITE A practice 'Upkeep' weapon attached to the bomb bay of Wing Commander Guy Gibson's Avro Type 464 (Provisioning) Lancaster, ED932/G AJ-G, at Manston, Kent, while conducting dropping trials off Reculver, 16 May 1943. (Photo by IWM via Getty Images)

Grand Slam bomb (of 22,000lb nominal weight, it actually weighed 22,400lb).

The largest weapon dropped by the RAF during World War II, it measured 25ft 5in long and contained 11,000lb of Torpex high explosive. It was designed to penetrate especially tough targets, typified by the German navy's reinforced concrete U-boat pens, which had roofs up to 35ft thick. A free-fall bomb, Grand Slam reached supersonic speed on its journey towards the ground; the weapon embedded itself deep in the target before exploding. The powerful shockwaves created by its detonation earned the Grand Slam its 'earthquake bomb' nickname.

The massive proportions of Wallis's earthquake bomb meant the only aircraft capable of carrying it was the Lancaster, albeit with a large amount of modification. The bomb bay doors were removed and alterations made to the bay, including the addition of a fairing at either end.

The prototype B.Mk I Special flew with all three turrets in place, but the nose and mid-upper turrets

LANCASTER B.MK I SPECIAL SPECIFICATION

(*Data as Mk I/III unless specified*)

Powerplant: 4 × Rolls-Royce Merlin 24 engines

Weight (loaded): 73,000lb (33,112kg)

Range (with Grand Slam): 1,650 miles (2,655km)

Service ceiling (with Grand Slam): 17,000ft

Defensive armament: 4 × Browning 0.303in machine guns in power-operated tail turret

Offensive armament: 1 × 22,000lb Grand Slam bomb

were soon removed to save weight and their positions faired over. This left only the four-gun tail turret as defensive armament, although this was later reduced to housing a pair of 0.5in Brownings. The combined weight of aircraft and bomb also required a strengthened undercarriage.

The Mk I Special's fuel load was reduced to 1,675Imp gal, restricting the aircraft to a range of 1,650 miles. This reduction in range did not affect the type's operational usefulness, since by the time it entered service in March 1945 the Allies were firmly ensconced in mainland Europe and the aircraft could reach all the targets allocated to it from European airfields.

Grand Slam challenged even the Lancaster, which was only capable of lifting the bomb to an altitude of 17,000ft, even after modification. This ceiling was lower than that which Wallis considered ideal for the weapon to achieve maximum penetration. Nonetheless, its results proved his concerns unfounded and 41 Grand Slams were dropped before the war's end.

LANCASTER B.MK VI

The B.Mk VI was an attempt to fit the Lancaster with the uprated Merlin 85/87 engine. Two airframes (DV170 and DV199), built by Metropolitan-Vickers at Trafford Park, were sent to Rolls-Royce for engine installations in June and July 1943. A third airframe, built by Avro at Newton Heath, JB675 was delivered to Rolls-Royce in November 1943 to become the first 'prototype' B.Mk VI.

LANCASTER B.MK VI SPECIFICATION

(Data as Mk I/III unless specified)

Powerplant: 4 × Rolls-Royce Merlin 85/87 engines

Following modification, it was delivered to the A&AEE at Boscombe Down for trials. It later served with four different squadrons, but flew only a single operational sortie before being transferred to the Royal Aircraft Establishment (RAE) at Farnborough.

A small number of Lancasters was converted to B.Mk VI configuration, serving mainly with No. 7 Sqn at RAF Oakington and No. 635 Sqn at RAF Downham Market, in the Pathfinder role.

The more powerful engines proved less reliable in service and this is probably why the B.Mk VI had been withdrawn from operations by November 1944.

LANCASTER B.MK I (FE)

The Lancaster B.Mk I (FE) was the result of 1944 RAF thinking in preparation for operations in the Far East. The Lancaster was to join the long-range US strategic bombing offensive against Japan until a replacement – the Avro Lincoln – was available.

Several Lancaster B.Mk I aircraft were taken from the production lines at Vickers-Armstrong and Armstrong Whitworth for storage at No. 38 Maintenance Unit (MU) at Llanlow. Here they awaited tropicalisation, ready for despatch to the Far East for service with 'Tiger Force', an RAF formation created for service against Japan. These aircraft were designated Lancaster B.Mk I (FE).

In view of the long distances involved in Pacific theatre operations, a number of suggestions were made concerning ways in which the Lancaster's range could be increased. One saw two Lancasters, HK541 and SW244, converted to carry large saddle tanks on their centre upper fuselage. These long-range fuel tanks were covered by a large fairing extending from the cockpit to just aft of the wing trailing edge, and necessitated removal of the mid-upper turret. They held 1,500Imp

LANCASTER B.MK I (FE) SPECIFICATION

(*Data as Mk I/III unless specified*)

Weights: Varied depending upon tropical equipment fit

Performance: Varied depending upon tropical equipment fit

Defensive armament: 2 × Browning 0.303in machine guns in power-operated FN5 nose turret; 4 × Browning 0.303in machine guns in power-operated FN20 tail turret

gal of fuel and increased the aircraft's all-up weight to 72,000lb.

HK541 underwent trials with the A&AEE at Boscombe Down before being sent to Mauripor, India for in-theatre trials in May 1944; SW244 followed in August 1945. Number 1577 Flight tested them and found their handling characteristics poor. The project was abandoned and the aircraft flown home for scrapping.

Another idea was to convert 600 Lancasters as aerial tankers. Inflight refuelling had been demonstrated before the war, although its application in military operations was relatively untried. At the end of 1944, trials began with a modified aircraft at the A&AEE at Boscombe Down, but the end of the war saw the project cancelled.

In the event, it was decided that Tiger Force would be equipped with tropicalised but otherwise standard Lancaster B.Mk I, III or VII aircraft. Their mid-upper turrets would be removed, enabling the FE aircraft to carry an additional 400Imp gal fuel tank in their bomb bay. The machines were also to be fitted with the best navigation equipment available, including Gee, Loran, Rebecca and H2S.

The atomic bomb attacks on Hiroshima and Nagasaki ended the war in the Pacific and Tiger Force disbanded in October 1945. The re-organised post-war Bomber Command continued operating 'standard' Lancasters while it awaited the new Lancaster B.Mk IV and B.Mk V, and the B.Mk I (FE) was retained for service in the Middle and Far East.

ABOVE TW878/TL-H was among the 16 No. 35 Sqn Lancaster B.Mk 1 (FE)s that took part in a US goodwill tour in August 1946. (Adam Tooby © Osprey Publishing)

LANCASTER B.MK VII (FE)

The Lancaster B.Mk VII was intended from the outset for Tiger Force. Austin Motors modified the prototype B.Mk VII, NN801, from Mk I standard, as the forerunner of the 230 aircraft it built at Longbridge.

The B.Mk VII was externally similar to the B.Mk I except for replacement of the FN50 mid-upper turret with a Martin frameless unit, moved forward to a position just aft of the wing trailing edge. The new position caused difficulty with crew movement fore and aft, but increased the ease of access and escape for the mid-upper gunner.

Supplies of the US-manufactured Martin turret were delayed and the first four Mk VIIs (NX548, NX589, NX603 and NX610) were fitted with the FN50 in the new position, along with the FN20 tail turret. These aircraft were classified as Lancaster B.Mk VII (interim). The Martin unit became available for the main production run, at which time the tail turret was also replaced, with the FN82 rear turret equipped, like the Martin unit, with two 0.5in guns.

All the B.Mk VII (FE) aircraft saw service overseas

LANCASTER B.MK VII (FE) SPECIFICATION

(Data as Mk I/III unless specified)

Weight (all-up): 72,000lb (32,659kg)

Defensive armament (initial four aircraft): 2 × Browning 0.303in machine guns each in power-operated FN5 nose and FN50 mid-upper turrets; 4 × Browning 0.303in machine guns in power-operated FN20 tail turret

Defensive armament (main production aircraft): 2 × Browning 0.303in machine guns in power-operated FN5 nose turret; 2 × Browning 0.5in machine guns each in power-operated frameless Martin mid-upper and FN82 tail turrets

before the end of World War II, except for NX558, which went to Avro for trials.

LANCASTER ASR/GR/MR.MK 3

The end of the war in Europe left the RAF with a gap in its inventory. It had largely depended on US types to fulfil Coastal Command's maritime requirements and these had been returned or disposed of under the terms of the Lend-Lease agreement under which they had been supplied. The RAF was thus left without maritime reconnaissance and long-range air/sea rescue (ASR) aircraft.

Coastal Command had used Lancasters for maritime reconnaissance during the war and although their crews had relied on visual surveillance since no radar was installed, the airframe had proven able to withstand the stresses associated with long-range maritime patrol.

Post-war, Cunliffe-Owen modified several Lancaster

LANCASTER ASR/GR/MR.MK 3 SPECIFICATION

(Data as Mk I/III unless specified)

Defensive armament: 2 × Browning 0.303in machine guns in power-operated FN5 nose turret; 4 × Browning 0.303in machine guns in power-operated FN20 tail turret

ABOVE A well-used Lancaster GR.Mk 3, SW336 of No. 38 Sqn. The window in the crew entry door was not present in other Lancaster marks. (Cody Images)

B.Mk IIIs from the RE, RF and SW serial blocks for the ASR role. The conversion removed the mid-upper turret and added external attachments to hold a lifeboat suspended under the bomb bay. A window was installed in each side of the fuselage forward of the tailplane for observation purposes. All the ASR conversions were fitted with H2S. Initially designated ASR.Mk III, these aircraft soon became ASR.Mk 3 machines under the RAF's post-war designation system.

The RAF struggled in the maritime role until 1947, when the ASR Lancasters were modified for general reconnaissance as GR.Mk 3 aircraft. These had airborne surface vessel (ASV) radar under their H2S radomes, while an aft-facing camera was installed in a pod under the rear turret. A change in role (and designation) occurred in 1950 when the aircraft were retitled MR for maritime reconnaissance, by which time Lincoln-style undercarriages had been fitted on some. The MR Lancaster soldiered on until the Shackleton arrived to replace it.

LANCASTER MK 1 (MODIFIED)

The Lancaster B.Mk 1 (modified) was in all technical respects identical to the standard B.Mk I. Under the terms of the Western Union Agreement of 1948, the Aéronavale (French naval air arm) received surplus Lancaster B.Mk I and B.Mk VII aircraft modified for maritime reconnaissance. Converted by Avro, all were designated as Lancaster Mk 1 (modified).

The modifications reflected peacetime requirements. The dorsal turret was removed and replaced by an escape hatch. Additional fuel tanks were fitted in the bomb bay and advanced mission equipment installed. All were allocated Aéronavale WK serials, the first, WK-01, being handed over in January 1952. In all, 32 Mk I and 22 Mk VII aircraft were modified.

LANCASTER B.MK IV AND B.MK V

The Lancaster B.Mk IV and B.Mk V were designed to meet Air Ministry requirement B.14/43. It called for a large bomber powered by four two-stage, two-speed Merlin engines. The new aircraft was expected to be capable of operating at altitudes up to 35,000ft and to have an all-up weight of 70,000lb.

In response, Roy Chadwick proposed a modified Lancaster airframe. An 8ft insert lengthened the fuselage and the nose was changed to a design based upon that of a modified unit trialled on Lancaster ED371. This accommodated the bomb aimer in a seated position, rather than in the prone position of previous Lancaster marks and about which Bomber Command had expressed some dissatisfaction. The new nose replaced the bomb aimer's blister with a framed, flat-panelled bomb-aiming blister and featured more capable equipment, as well as an improved turret.

ABOVE An Aéronavale Lancaster in typical overall white finish. Note the lack of armament in the turrets. (Cody Images)

The Lancaster wing was extended with new outer sections, increasing span to 120ft and enabling the aircraft to meet the performance requirements laid down in B.14/43. Wing tank fuel capacity was increased to 3,500Imp gal.

Avro equipped the B.Mk IV and B.Mk V with a new nose turret mounting a pair of Browning 0.5in machine guns and a new tail turret with two similar weapons. More significantly, the dorsal position featured another new turret, positioned just aft of the wing trailing edge, holding a pair of 20mm Hispano cannon.

In order to cope with the aircraft's increased weight, the undercarriage was replaced by one of more robust design; the bomb bay was also modified.

Known as the Avro Type 694, the design was expressed as the Lancaster B.Mk IV with Merlin 85 engines and Lancaster B.Mk V with Merlin 68A engines. It resembled the Lancaster in general layout,

LANCASTER B.MK IV AND V SPECIFICATION

Powerplant (B.Mk IV): 4 × Rolls-Royce Merlin 85 engines

Powerplant (B.Mk V): 4 × Packard Merlin 68A engines

Length: 78ft 3in (23.9m)

Height: 17ft (5.2m)

Wingspan: 120ft (36.6m)

Wing area: 1,421sqft (132m²)

Weight (B.Mk IV, all-up): 75,000lb (34,019kg)

Maximum speed at 12,000ft (B.Mk IV): 319mph

(513km/h)

Range (B.Mk IV): 1,470 miles (4,070km)

Range (with 12,000lb load): 1,700 miles (2,366km)

Service ceiling (B.Mk IV): 30,000ft

Defensive armament (B.Mk IV): 2 × 0.5in Browning machine guns each in power-operated Boulton Paul 'F' nose and 'D' tail turret; 2 × 20mm Hispano cannon in Bristol 17 mid-upper turret

Offensive armament: Up to 14,000lb (6,350kg) of bombs and other freefall ordnance

but was actually a very different machine. Avro requested a name change to reflect the fundamentally new design, but Bomber Command was keen to keep the Lancaster moniker.

In June 1944, however, the company suggested three possible new names for the Type 694, Sandringham, Stafford and Lincoln. Air Vice-Marshal J. D. Breakey, Assistant Chief of the Air Staff (Technical Requirements)

commented that Lincoln was appropriate, since it not only reflected the current convention of naming bombers after British cities, but also reflected the area in which the majority of Bomber Command's Lancaster stations were located. The name was officially approved in August, the Lancaster B.Mk IV becoming the Lincoln B.Mk I and the Lancaster B.Mk V the Lincoln B.Mk II.

Bomber Command did not receive the Lincoln for

service until after World War II, even though it had been designed from the outset for service in the Far East. The first prototype, PW925, had its maiden flight in June 1944, but developments in the global conflict reduced the urgency with which the aircraft was placed into service.

The need for large numbers of bombers disappeared after the war ended and many Lincolns were cancelled.

Despite this, more than 500 were built, and the aircraft served the Royal Air Force well into the 1950s; it also flew with the Argentine and Australian air forces. The RAF retired its last Lincoln from service in 1963.

MISSION EQUIPMENT
GEE AND LORAN
Bomber Command's was a difficult mission. The idea

of sending massed bomber fleets against strategic targets had seemed bright and simple pre-war, when heavily armed formations were imagined penetrating enemy air defences with immunity as they navigated in to attack targets with pinpoint accuracy.

The reality was far away from this 1930s vision. Bomber Command found its aircraft vulnerable as soon as they met modern fighters, while night fighters, and especially anti-aircraft (AA) guns, or *Flak*, took a heavy toll right through to the war's end. Finding targets proved extremely difficult in typical Northern European overcast conditions, and long-distance navigation challenged all but the finest crews.

But science came to Bomber Command's assistance and a series of technologies was developed to help its bombers reach their targets and, to a degree, keep them safe. Among these, Gee was designed to assist navigation and permit 'blind' bombing when the target was not visible to the bomb aimer. It relied on reception of signals from a series of ground stations, the master (A) and two

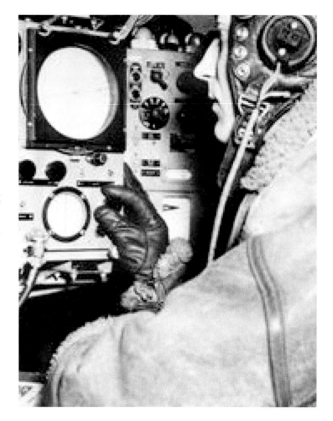

slaves (B and C), along a 200-mile (322km) baseline. The time difference between receiving signals from A and B, and B and C was displayed on a unit in the aircraft. The navigator could calculate a ground position by referencing the display to a 'Gee Chart', which gave a result accurate to within 5.5 miles (8.9km). Only a limited number of aircraft were fitted with Gee and they typically led bomber streams to targets within the system's operating range, dropping their bomb load, which mainly comprised incendiaries, to mark the target.

The US developed the long-range navigation (Loran) system to guide aircraft flying over the sea. It used pairs of transmitting stations that gave the navigator a single position at a time, the navigator alternating between stations on 1-minute cycles to 'get a fix'. It was used from 1944, when Gee sets were modified to allow them to switch between Gee and Loran.

OPPOSITE The cathode ray tube Plan Position Indicator (PPI) and controls of an H2S radar system being operated by the navigator in a Lancaster bomber, circa 1944. (© IWM E(MOS) 1436)

OBOE

Oboe was the most accurate of the navigation systems used during World War II. It was required because Gee could be, and was, jammed, although in the technological game played between British and German scientists, Oboe was eventually jammed too. Designed in 1941, it was based on two ground stations. The first, called 'cat', sent out a dot-dash signal, the second, called 'mouse', sent out a release signal, both on the same wavelength but at different pulse frequencies.

A repeater in the aircraft responded to both frequencies, allowing each station to measure the aircraft's range. If it was on track, the pilot heard a steady tone in his headset, otherwise he adjusted course as necessary. The system was only used in the target area.

H2S

H2S was essentially an airborne interception radar installed under the aircraft to point at the ground. Returning pulses were displayed on the Plan Position Indicator, a cathode ray tube in the navigator's position. H2S generated a radar map of the terrain ahead of the aircraft and that over which it was flying, enabling the navigator to get a fix on where the aircraft was. The display required considerable skill to interpret accurately, but on the plus side H2S was not affected by weather, cloud or jamming and was completely independent of ground stations.

On the Lancaster, the H2S set was installed in a large, clear perspex blister on the underside of the fuselage just aft of the bomb bay. The blister was sometimes painted in the underside colour for the forward two thirds of its length, with the rear third left unpainted. The first three Lancasters fitted with H2S were B.Mk IIIs JB352, JB355 and JB356, in November 1943. The primary flaw in H2S emerged when the Luftwaffe began equipping its night fighters with Naxos, a system that homed on H2S emissions.

GEE-H

Gee-H, or simply G-H, was effectively an Oboe set working in reverse, the aircraft transmitting the signals to mobile ground stations to acquire a navigational fix. More aircraft could use the Gee-H system simultaneously, but accuracy depended heavily on the crew's ability. The system was first used on the night of 3/4 November 1943 during a raid on Dusseldorf. By October 1944, one third of No. 3 Group's Lancasters were fitted with the system.

ELECTRONIC WARFARE

A number of electronic warfare (EW) systems were fitted to Lancasters during World War II. Some were restricted to aircraft serving No. 100 Group, which was dedicated to delivering electronic countermeasures (ECM) against German defensive equipment, while others were fitted to Main Force Lancasters.

All Main Force Lancasters employed Window, later known as chaff, which consisted of aluminium foil strips cut to precise lengths so that they would interfere with German ground radar by generating multiple false targets. Window was initially dropped through the aircraft's flare chute by hand, but a Window distribution box was later fitted to the fuselage side.

Another 'jamming' device was Tinsel. Also carried by Main Force Lancasters, it used a microphone fixed into an engine nacelle. From this, engine noise was broadcast on the frequencies used by night fighters to communicate with their ground stations, making it impossible for the fighter to be guided to an intercept position.

Mandrel was also installed on Main Force Lancasters, producing a signal that saturated German *Freya* early-warning radar sets.

Another Main Force system, Monica comprised an aft-facing radar set to detect approaching night fighters. Lancasters fitted with Monica featured an aerial under their rear turret, but Monica was removed after it was discovered that the night fighters were using *Flensburg* sets, which homed on its emissions.

Airborne Cigar (ABC) was initially fitted to No. 101 Squadron Lancasters. It comprised three transmitters and a receiver, and required a Special Duties Operator. A German speaker, the operator manned the ABC set, identifying radio traffic between the ground stations and night fighter crews and jamming their frequencies.

Airborne Cigar-equipped Lancasters were equipped with three aerials, two on the upper fuselage and one under the nose.

COMBAT OPERATIONS

The Lancaster arrived with Bomber Command at a difficult time for the organisation. A survey of individual aircraft bombing photographs revealed that even the best crews were achieving very much lower accuracy figures than had been assumed. Overall, only one in four crews claiming to have bombed a target had got within five miles of it, while in cloudy conditions the figure dropped to one in fifteen. Even on clear summer nights, fewer than half of the crews dropped their bombs within five miles of their target. Figures for targets in Germany were slightly worse.

Following the report, AOC-in-C Bomber Command Air Marshal Sir Richard Peirse switched the focus of his offensive to easier, lower priority targets, less well protected by *Flak*, searchlights, fighters and the Ruhr's

OPPOSITE Three Avro Lancaster B.Mk Is of No. 44 Sqn based at Waddington, Lincolnshire, flying above the clouds. (Photo by Royal Air Force Official Photographer/ IWM via Getty Images)

natural defence of mist and haze. But even against these targets, it was clear that crews were becoming less willing to press home their attacks, and many suspected that the Command was beginning to suffer a crisis of confidence.

Nor were these modest results being obtained cheaply. During a four-month period from 7/8 July to 10 November 1941, Bomber Command had lost 526 aircraft – equivalent to its entire frontline strength! Aircraft were relatively easy to replace, but the losses of trained crews presented a much more difficult problem. Air Marshal Peirse was ordered to scale down operations while the future of the bomber offensive was examined and debated.

Peirse had done his best with the limited and inadequate resources at his disposal, presiding over a Command with obsolete or unsuitable aircraft, and with insufficient navigation equipment to achieve the degree of bombing accuracy required. It had lost many of its most senior and highly skilled aircrew, and, although he had been provided with 'shoddy tools', Peirse shouldered the blame for the Command's failure. He was removed from his post on 8 January 1942 and temporarily replaced by the AOC No. 3 Group, Air Vice Marshal J. E. A. Baldwin, while a new strategy was formulated.

The decision to continue the strategic bombing campaign was made largely on pragmatic and political grounds. With Britain's new Russian ally fighting for its life in the east, Bomber Command was the only means by which the RAF could take the fight to the enemy, and was thus the only means by which Churchill could 'hold up his head' in dealings with Stalin.

The bomber enthusiasts exploited the fact that Bomber Command was supposedly the only arm of Britain's armed forces hitting the Germans in the west (conveniently forgetting the army in the Western Desert, and the joint forces battling in the Atlantic) and drew up a plan for a revolutionary new bomber offensive. This entailed a programme of 'continuous attack' against 43 leading German industrial cities and their combined population of 15 million.

Such attacks would be against the cities themselves, not only the factories within them, and it was calculated that a bomber force of 4,000 aircraft would produce complete collapse within six months. Churchill rejected the plan, but tacitly approved the switch from an attempt at precision bombing to a deliberate area bombing strategy.

On 14 February 1942, Bomber Command received a directive confirming the change of emphasis. This stated: 'The Primary Objective of your operation should now be focused on the morale of the enemy civil population, and in particular of the industrial workers.' In a subsequent letter, Chief of the Air Staff Portal sought confirmation that henceforth 'aiming points are to be built up areas, and not, for instance, the dockyards or aircraft factories.'

OPPOSITE Air Chief Marshal Sir Arthur Harris, nicknamed 'Bomber' Harris. (Photo by © Hulton-Deutsch Collection/CORBIS/ Corbis via Getty)

The War Cabinet and Air Ministry formulated the new policy, Bomber Command having little input. Neither did the Command's new AOC-in-C – Air Chief Marshal Sir Arthur Harris – appointed eight days later, although his fierce approval and championing of the policy made many think it was his own.

Harris inherited a Command in reasonably good shape. The hopeless Manchester, ageing Hampden and prehistoric Whitley would all be gone by the end of 1942, replaced by Halifaxes, Stirlings and Lancasters. Aircraft were also being equipped with the Gee navigation system, which enabled them to find closer targets, including Bremen, Emden, the Rhineland, the Ruhr and Wilhelmshaven, and which was a powerful aid in helping lost bombers recover to Britain.

Harris nurtured considerable enthusiasm for incendiaries and devoted single-minded attention to concentrating raids into the shortest possible timeframe in order to overwhelm the defences and emergency services. Under his instruction, Bomber Command used high-explosive bombs to blow off roofs and blow

ABOVE No. 44 (Rhodesia) Sqn received its first Lancasters on Christmas Eve 1941, trading in its twin-engined Hampdens. L7578, shown here in flight over the Lincolnshire countryside on 14 April 1942 while practising for a low-level attack on the M.A.N. diesel engineering works at Augsburg, remained with the unit only briefly, before being assigned to No. 97 Sqn. (Photo by No. 44 (Rhodesia) Squadron, Royal Air Force/ IWM via Getty Images)

out windows, block roads with rubble, and hinder the fire brigades, while dropping huge numbers of incendiaries that took hold in the roofless, windowless buildings. 'It's easier to burn a city down than it is to blow it up,' he once famously remarked.

When he took over the reins at Bomber Command's High Wycombe headquarters, Harris (known to the press and public as 'Bomber' Harris, and 'Butch' to his intimates) had two Lancaster units in the process of forming. Number 44 Sqn had received its first aircraft on Christmas Eve 1941, while No. 97 Sqn followed in January 1942. The Lancaster had almost flown its first operation (a mining mission of Aas Fjord, aimed at bottling up the German battleship *Tirpitz*) on 25 January, but had been prevented from doing so by the unserviceability of the planned forward operating base at Wick.

Number 97 Squadron was loaned the first prototype, BT308, on 10 January to begin conversion, and soon began receiving production aircraft.

Lancaster operations finally began on 3/4 March, when No. 44 Sqn despatched four aircraft to 'garden' (mine) 'Yams' and 'Rosemary' (the approach to Heligoland, and an area further north), each with four 'vegetables' (mines). A week later, on 10/11 March, No. 44 Sqn contributed two aircraft to a raid on Essen, and sent another against Cologne three nights later. Number 97 Sqn began Lancaster operations on 20 March, despatching six aircraft on a 'gardening' mission at 'Willows' (Swinemünde, in the Baltic).

The first operational Lancaster loss occurred on 24/25 March, when No. 44 Sqn's Flight Sergeant Warren-Smith failed to return from a mining sortie. The largest-scale Lancaster mission to date occurred on 25/26 March when seven Lancasters drawn from both squadrons, and equipped with Gee were sent out as part of a 254-aircraft raid on Essen. Although 181 crews claimed to have bombed the city, many were drawn off by a well-constructed decoy, and German records showed that only nine bombs and 700 incendiaries fell on the town, destroying one house, damaging two more and killing five people. Bomber Command lost nine aircraft in achieving this modest success.

By the end of March the Command had received 54 Lancasters, ten of them going to a third unit, No. 207 Sqn, forming that same month.

AUGSBURG

The Lancaster gave Bomber Command an aircraft Harris believed capable of attacking any target in Germany. By April 1942, Nos 44 and 97 Sqns were flying together at low level, and rumours abounded that a special mission was on the horizon. These gained strength when No. 44 Sqn, led by Sqn Ldr John Nettleton, and No. 97 Sqn, led by Sqn Ldr John Sherwood, undertook a special training flight, in which both squadrons independently flew to the south coast, where they joined up to transit north and carry out a simulated 'attack' on Inverness.

The crews believed they were going to be detailed against German warships, but when they were briefed at their own bases on 17 April they learned that they were to attack the Maschinenfabrik Augsburg-Nurnburg Aktiengesellschaft factory at Augsburg, in southern Germany, which was producing diesel engines for U-boats. Augsburg was 1,000 miles away, requiring Bomber Command's deepest penetration into Germany so far.

The plan called for six aircraft from each squadron to cross the Channel west of Le Havre and transit south at low level, before turning east to pass south of Paris. They would then head towards Munich, as if the raid was targeted there, before turning north to attack Augsburg.

The target required precision bombing since it was a particularly small site, and it was therefore decided that the attack would take place at low level in the last minutes of daylight, allowing the bombers to return under cover of darkness. Each Lancaster would carry only four 1,000lb general-purpose (GP) bombs, fitted with time-delay fuses. Diversionary bombing and fighter sweeps were scheduled for the afternoon to divert Luftwaffe fighters from the Augsburg flight.

At 15:00 hours the 12 Lancasters took off and formed into four flights of three aircraft each. As they crossed the French coast, the diversionary raids had brought the Luftwaffe up and a group of Messerschmitt

OPPOSITE The bomb load most commonly used for area bombing raids (codeword 'Usual') in the bomb bay of an Avro Lancaster of No. 57 Sqn at Scampton Lincolnshire. 'Usual' consisted of a 4,000 impact-fused HC bomb ('cookie'), and 12 Small Bomb Containers (SBCs) each loaded with incendiaries, in this case, 236 x 4lb incendiary sticks.

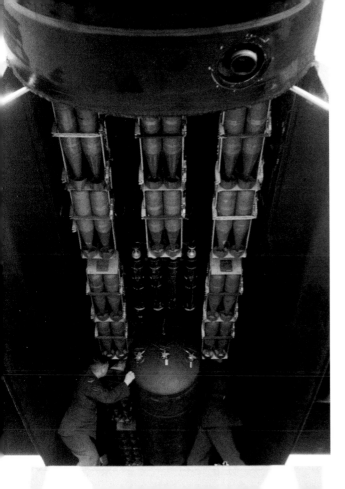

Bf 109 fighters returning from an interception spotted the last section of Lancasters. They caught No. 44 Sqn's rear flight and immediately shot down the Lancaster flown by Warrant Officer 'Joe' Beckett DFM.

Six Bf 109s turned on the second Lancaster, flown by Warrant Officer 'Bert' Crum DFM. Both its port engines were soon hit and burning, the aircraft crashing into a field. The last Lancaster in the section, flown by Flight Lieutenant 'Nick' Sandford DFC, was also shot down.

Next the fighters turned on Nettleton's lead section. His number three, flown by Sergeant 'Dusty' Rhodes, was shot down. Both Nettleton's Lancaster and his number two, piloted by Flying Officer 'Ginger' Garwell DFM, came under repeated attack and were hit a number of times, but the Messerschmitts ran short of fuel and were forced to disengage. The two flights of No. 97 Sqn were unmolested, despite being only two miles away, and the surviving pair of No. 44 Sqn Lancasters continued to Augsburg without further incident.

Nettleton pressed home a determined attack at Augsburg. *Flak* hit Garwell's aircraft on the run-in to the target and it crashed moments after releasing its bombs. Number 97 Squadron reached the target after Nettleton, by which time the defences were fully alerted.

Sherwood led the first flight in and was met by a barrage of dense AA fire. All the flight's Lancasters bombed, but Sherwood's was seen to explode on impact with the ground. The rear section, led by Flight Lieutenant 'Jock' Penman, began its attack, but the German gunners had by then established the exact line and altitude of the run-in.

The number two aircraft, flown by Flying Officer Ernest Deverill DFC, was hit repeatedly, putting its gun turrets out of action, causing the hydraulic oil in the mid-upper turret to catch fire and setting fire to the starboard inner engine. The third aircraft also caught fire on the

RIGHT The bomb load used for industrial demolition (Bomber Command executive codeword 'Abnormal'), loaded in the bomb-bay of a Lancaster of No. 9 Sqn at Bardney, Lincolnshire, before a night raid on Stettin, Germany, 5 January 1944. 'Abnormal' consisted of fourteen 1,000lb MC high-explosive bombs. (Photo by FO S. A. Devon/ IWM via Getty Images)

run-in, although Warrant Officer Tommy Mycock DFC managed to keep his aircraft steady long enough for the bombs to be released before it exploded.

The five remaining aircraft turned for the long journey home. It passed without incident, although Nettleton landed at Squire's Gate near Blackpool after running short of fuel. The only survivor from the six No. 44 Sqn aircraft had returned safely. The four remaining No. 97 Sqn aircraft had all landed by midnight. Deverill's Lancaster was written off immediately, so severe was its damage.

The raid had been successful in so much as production at the factory was disrupted for several weeks. But of the 85 men who had set out that afternoon, 49 were missing and only 12 of those survived to become prisoners of war. Nettleton was awarded the Victoria Cross for his outstanding leadership; the rest of his crew were awarded DFCs and DFMs.

REGULAR WORK

Meanwhile, seven Lancasters had participated in a raid on Hamburg on 8/9 April. Eight Lancasters also joined the attack on Essen on 10/11 April, during which as few as six of the 172 aircraft that bombed managed to hit the city.

Further raids involving Lancasters were carried out against Rostock over 23–27 April, the last of which prompted Goebbels to coin the phrase terrorangriff (terror raid). Less successful attempts followed against Stuttgart, Warnemünde and Mannheim in May, and the Gnome-Rhône engine factory at Paris Gennevilliers.

But for every successful raid there were several failures, and Bomber Command's future remained under threat. What was needed was a morale-boosting spectacular, which Harris provided in the form of the first Thousand Bomber Raid.

THOUSAND BOMBER RAIDS

This was an incredible achievement, not least because Harris could call on only about 400 aircraft and trained crews from his frontline units, forcing him to boost numbers with aircraft and crews from the Operational Training Units (OTUs). The latter not only sent instructors – of the 208 aircraft provided by No. 91 Group, for example, 49 took off captained by student pilots. Harris had originally planned on using up to 250 bombers from Coastal Command and a handful from Flying Training Command.

The latter organisation initially offered 50 Wellingtons, but most of these were inadequately equipped for night bombing, and in the end the Command provided only four Vickers bombers for the first Thousand Bomber Raid. The Admiralty, unwilling to participate in what it saw as a public relations exercise, forbade Coastal Command participation altogether, fearful of losing control of its handful of long-range aircraft.

Nonetheless, Harris launched 1,047 aircraft, including 73 Lancasters on his first Thousand Bomber Raid, against Cologne, on 30 May 1942. The magnificent cathedral city was Harris's second choice, but poor weather three nights running ruled out his preferred target of Hamburg. Cologne's relative proximity to Bomber Command's East Anglian bases, and its position on the river Rhine (highly visible to H2S, and within Gee range), made it a common 'fallback' target when weather or heavy losses ruled out hitting more distant cities.

According to Bomber Command records, 868 aircraft attacked the primary target, dropping 1,455 tons of bombs (mainly incendiaries), destroying 3,330 buildings and damaging many others. The raid killed between 469 and 486 Germans, most of them civilians, and injured 5,027 more. Some 45,132 people were 'bombed out' of their homes, and an estimated 150,000 fled the city.

A single Lancaster was shot down, together with 40 other RAF bombers, and it was calculated that casualty rates reduced as the German defences were progressively overwhelmed. Churchill had been prepared for the loss of up to 100 aircraft, and thus saw the raid as a great success.

While the press and public seized upon the sheer number of aircraft involved, the tactics used were even more significant. During the war's early raids, 100 aircraft had taken up to four hours to attack a typical target. But the 'bomber stream' used in the Thousand Bomber Raids funnelled the participating aircraft through the target in an astonishing 90 minutes.

This ensured the aircraft passed through the minimum number of German night-fighter 'boxes', reducing the chances of interception, and also ensured that *Flak* and searchlight defences at the target would be overwhelmed. German airspace was divided into a network of night-fighter boxes, each controlled by a single ground controlled intercept (GCI) controller. He could only direct a maximum of six intercepts per hour, meaning that if 1,000 aircraft passed through his 'box' in one hour, only six could potentially be intercepted.

Passing the maximum number of aircraft over the target in the minimum timescale also ensured that fire brigades on the ground would be overwhelmed by the quantity of incendiaries dropped. Harris had originally planned to launch a couple of Thousand Bomber Raids during every suitable moon period, but in the event, there would only be three of these 'maximum effort' attacks.

Harris kept his Cologne strike force together for a follow-up attack on Essen two nights later on 1/2 June. Although billed as another Thousand Bomber Raid, only 956 aircraft could be assembled, and 74 of these were Lancasters – 31 bombers failed to return, including four Lancasters. Haze or thin cloud cover made it difficult to find the target, and most bombers failed to attack Essen, which suffered the loss of 11 houses, 15 civilian dead and a burned-out PoW working camp.

Smaller raids followed against Essen, Bremen and Emden in June, to little effect. On 25/26, Bremen became the target of the third and final Thousand Bomber Raid. Bomber Command sent out 960 aircraft, with 102 Coastal Command Hudsons and Wellingtons, and five Army Co-operation Command Blenheims taking the total to 1,067. Lancasters accounted for ten per cent of the Bomber Command force, with 96 aircraft sortied.

The force transited the target area in only 65 minutes. Bremen was within Gee range, so the leading aircraft were able to bomb despite cloud cover, achieving a degree of accuracy. A strengthening wind fanned the flames and 572 houses were destroyed (with 6,108 more damaged) and 85 Bremeners killed.

Nevertheless, the Germans were convinced that only 80 aircraft had bombed, and claimed 52 of these shot down. Subsequent BBC broadcasts claiming that 'a thousand bombers' had been despatched were taken as propaganda aimed at making the losses more palatable to the British public. In fact, 44 aircraft had been shot down in the target area, four more falling on their way back across the North Sea. In absolute terms, this was Bomber Command's heaviest loss of the war so far, although in percentile terms the loss was relatively light, at five per cent.

Bremen was attacked again on 27/28 June by 144 aircraft, including 24 Lancasters, on 29/30 June by 253 aircraft, including 64 Lancasters, and on 2/3 July by 325 aircraft, including 53 Lancasters. Bomber Command losses on all three nights totalled 33 aircraft, including two Lancasters. The second raid, on 29/30 June, marked the first occasion on which four-engined bombers accounted for more than half the aircraft sent out on a large-scale raid, with 145 of the 253 aircraft being 'heavies'.

On 11 July, Bomber Command struck the U-boat yards at Danzig, its most distant target yet. Some 44 Lancasters sortied, of which 24 bombed and two more were shot down in the target area.

The Lancaster's next major raid was against Duisburg on 13/14 July. The attack achieved little, and ten aircraft failed to return. The 194 aircraft despatched included 13 Lancasters, one of which was lost.

Things went better on 19/20 July, when 99 heavies attacked the Vulkan U-boat works at Vegesack. The target was covered by cloud and the force bombed using Gee, and although all bombs missed their target, they did completely destroy two storehouses full of military equipment in nearby Bremen, and burned down a wooden-hutted military camp. None of the 28

Lancasters were lost, although three of 40 Halifaxes failed to return.

In late July, Duisburg, Hamburg and Saarbrücken were the targets of a series of raids, the last being the most destructive. Düsseldorf became the target at the end of the month, marking the first time that more than 100 Lancasters were sent out against a single target. Two Avro bombers were among the 29 aircraft that failed to return.

Duisburg was again the target on 6/7 August, but of the 216 accuracy was poor and five aircraft were lost. Ösnabruck and Mainz were attacked later that month for heavy damage, with low aircraft losses.

Bomber Command's last major attack before the Pathfinder Force became operational was on 17 August, 131-aircraft attacking Düsseldorf and causing little damage, although four bombers were lost.

THE PATHFINDERS

Although Harris had preferred to extend current tactics rather than creating a specialist force to improve bombing accuracy, he eventually relented and agreed to create a specialist Pathfinder Force (PFF) to find and mark targets. Harris selected one of his best leaders, Group Captain Donald Bennett, to lead it. Formed on 11 August 1942 and headquartered at RAF Warton, the PFF initially comprised squadrons from each of the bomber groups, including No. 83 Sqn on Lancasters.

It began operations on the night of 18/19 August when it marked *Flensburg* for the Main Force. The raid was not a great start, since the forecast winds were in error and 16 of the 31 Pathfinders bombed north of the town. The second raid, on Frankfurt, was also disappointing as cloud obscured the city, but the third, on Kassel, proved more successful.

Bennett identified a number of issues and it was only a matter of time before equipment and tactics would produce better results. Oboe and H2S were available by the end of the year, but there were no Lancasters to replace No. 83 Sqn's losses while Nos 49 and 9 squadrons were re-equipping. The mixed PFF fleet also created issues, its aircraft operating at different altitudes and ground speeds, and while PFF losses were expected be higher than those of the Main Force regardless of aircraft type, the Lancaster was considered the more survivable platform.

On 28/29 August the Pathfinders marked Nuremberg using newly developed target indicators, and the 159 aircraft despatched caused considerable damage, especially to the wooden *Kraft durch Freude* ('Strength through Joy') town, south of the city, which burned down. Number 106 Sqn dropped two 8,000lb blast bombs, adding to the devastation. Casualties were heavy, with 23 aircraft lost, including four of 71 Lancasters.

A 4/5 September attack on Bremen saw the Pathfinders split between 'illuminators', which lit up the target area with white flares, 'visual markers' that dropped coloured flares on the aim point and 'backers up', which dropped incendiaries on these marked aim points. The 251-aircraft raid caused heavy damage and 124 people were killed, although with 12 aircraft lost, including a Lancaster, the result was a costly one.

The Pathfinders used new 'Pink Pansie' target indicators for the first time during a 10/11 September raid on Düsseldorf. They seemed to bring about greater accuracy, although, with a 7.1 per cent loss rate, including five Lancasters and 20 Wellingtons, the Command was continuing down the road to complete annihilation.

On 23/24 September, No. 5 Group mounted an all-Lancaster raid, numbering 83 aircraft, on the town of Wismar and the nearby Dornier factory. Major damage and heavy casualties were inflicted, but four aircraft were lost.

LE CREUSOT

When Harris received orders to attack the French Schneider armament factory at Le Creusot, they presented him with a problem. He had little compunction against inflicting civilian casualties while attacking German targets, but was naturally

OPPOSITE A gaggle of at least 47 Lancasters (of a total force of 88) roars over the riverside town of Montrichard, en route to Schneider's Le Creusot works. (Cody Images)

concerned about collateral damage when attacking targets in occupied France. The Pathfinders were not yet accurate enough to ensure the degree of precision required, and Harris reluctantly accepted that the only option was a set-piece daylight raid by low-flying Lancasters.

Following the Augsburg example, the raid was launched in the early afternoon, so the force bombed in daylight (to ensure accuracy), but returned under cover of darkness. Nine units offered a total of 94 Lancasters for the 17 October raid. They set out for France in a gaggle, staying below 1,000ft to avoid detection by enemy radar. The Lancasters, led by Wing Commander Leonard Slee of No. 49 Sqn, crossed the French coast at 300ft close to Nantes, and looped around Tours en route to the target.

Nearing their objective, the nine squadrons (five aircraft had turned back early) fanned out and climbed to 4,000ft for their bombing runs, while six aircraft (two each from Nos 106, 9 and 61 Sqns, led by Wing Commander Guy Gibson) pushed on to bomb the Henri Paul transformer station at Montchanin, six miles further south.

These aircraft attacked in line astern from a nominal 500ft, although Hopgood's aircraft was damaged by the blast from his own bombs at 150ft and Corr's aircraft crashed in the target area, almost certainly due to the same cause. A No. 57 Sqn Lancaster was damaged when it flushed out a covey of partridges on the return trip, several of the birds smashing the windscreen and injuring the flight engineer. But apart from Corr's machine, all aircraft returned home safely. The plant was put out of action for more than three weeks, while repair work disrupted production for more than eight months.

WINTER BOMBING

Sixteen Lancasters failed to return during November despite the onset of winter weather, and an inevitable slackening of the offensive. Bomber Command switched some of its offensive focus towards Italy, sending four major raids across the Alps to Genoa and four to Turin. On 28/29 November, Gibson's and another No. 106 Sqn crew each took an 8,000lb bomb to Turin. Apart from these attacks, the only large-scale raids were against Hamburg and Stuttgart. Losses on the Italian missions were small, with three 'no loss' attacks.

In December the campaign against Turin continued, and major raids also struck at Duisburg, Frankfurt, Mannheim and Munich. The month saw the loss of 26 Lancasters. Results against the German targets were disappointing, but the three attacks against Turin were more successful and with relatively light losses.

SHIP-BUSTING

In April 1942, Nos 44 and 97 Sqns mounted seven-aircraft detachments to RAF Lossiemouth, near Elgin. On 27 April, six aircraft from each unit were despatched to attack *Tirpitz* as it lay at anchor at Trondheim. Few aircraft sighted the target on their first run, and a second pass brought no success. Eleven Lancasters returned from the mission, while four of 31 Halifaxes despatched against the same target failed to return. A second attempt the following night was no more successful.

Losses of Allied ships in the Atlantic continued to be a source of great concern. Coastal Command's AOC-in-C, Air Chief Marshal Sir Philip Joubert, was convinced that Britain could not survive for more than a year unless shipping losses were staunched, and that in order to halt the flow, his Command required more aircraft.

At the beginning of 1942, Joubert demanded the immediate transfer of six Wellington squadrons, with the provision of 81 Liberators and/or Fortresses in the longer term. Bomber Command was tardy in responding to the demand and released only a few tired Whitleys. Meanwhile, the U-boats began to improve their kill/loss ratio, and spent more time in the mid-Atlantic, out of range of all but the Liberators of No. 120 Sqn. This made it even more important to interdict them as they transited the Bay of Biscay, and for Bomber Command to protect shipping close to the coast, thus freeing all available Coastal Command aircraft for longer-range missions.

In June 1942, Bomber Command temporarily lost half of the longest-serving and most experienced of its seven Lancaster units when five No. 44 Sqn Lancasters were detached to Nutts Corner in County Antrim, Northern Ireland, for the second half of the month. The detachment attacked two submarines during its brief stint, with Flight Lieutenant T. P. C. Barlow DFC sinking the second.

The next Bomber Command Lancaster unit attached to Coastal Command was No. 61 Sqn, which sent eight aircraft and 12 crews to RAF St Eval, Cornwall, on 16 July for a five-week period. Remarkably, the unit scored a U-boat kill on its first sortie from St Eval, but claimed no further successes. The Lancasters suffered several engine failures, however. Finally, on 19 August, three failed to return from sorties against *Corunna*, a German blockade-runner, and *Flak* damaged another. Number 50 Sqn joined the cat-and-mouse game with *Corunna* the next day, when No. 61 Sqn lost a fourth aircraft.

Harris used the episode to justify his opposition to the 'diversion' of resources to 'irrelevant side-shows', pointing out that 12 No. 61 Sqn aircraft had mounted 96 patrols, totalling 878 hours, with the loss of four aircraft and 28 aircrew, while achieving 'only' the destruction of a single U-boat.

Bomber Command's record against the Kriegsmarine was poor up to that point in the war, having failed to stop the battleships *Scharnhorst* and *Gneisenau*, and the battlecruiser *Prinz Eugen*, as they escaped in the infamous 'Channel Dash' on 12 February 1942, and inflicted little damage on *Tirpitz*, despite numerous attempts to sink it. Part of the problem was the lack of suitable weapons, although various establishments had been working on a range of possible solutions for some months.

The most promising was the Capital Ship Bomb, a 5,600lb monster with a hollow (shaped) charge warhead. Described as looking 'like an elongated turnip', it was intended to penetrate an armoured deck before exploding and blowing out the ship's bottom.

In the Admiralty's eyes the most alarming German

warship was the aircraft carrier *Graf Zeppelin*, nearing completion in the Polish port of Gdynia, where the ships involved in the Channel Dash were also believed to be 'holed up'. Gdynia thus became the natural target for the first and only raid using the new Capital Ship Bomb, four of which had by then been constructed.

Bomber Command detailed Gibson's No. 106 Sqn to carry out the mission, ordering six crews to train for the still unspecified operation, and directing that six aircraft should be modified to carry the weapon. The new bombs were incredibly expensive and difficult to produce, and one was used in ballistics trials that showed it had an extremely irregular and unpredictable trajectory that would make accurate aiming all but impossible, except from very low level. In this context, even 1,000ft was regarded as too high.

It was decided that dropping the new weapons from 1,000ft would entail an unacceptable degree of risk to the Lancaster crews and the bomb was to be dropped from 6,000ft. On the night of 26/27 July 1942, three No. 106 Sqn Lancasters, captained by Gibson, Whamond and Hopgood, were despatched against Gdynia, which they found covered by a veil of haze and mist.

They remained in the target area for about an hour, despite heavy *Flak*, and caught fleeting glimpses of two capital ships. After about a dozen bombing runs, all three aircraft had dropped their weapons, but all missed – Gibson's by a reported 400 yards. The aircraft involved had staggered into the air at an all-up weight of 67,000lb, an astonishing 7,000lb above the aircraft's authorised maximum take-off weight.

The modifications to the six Lancaster B.Mk Is also enabled them to carry the new 8,000lb High Capacity (HC) bomb, and the unit began operations with it on 31 July/1 August, initially against Düsseldorf, and later Nuremberg and Turin.

1943 – ONWARDS TO BERLIN

'Bomber' Harris later described 1942 as marking a 'preliminary phase', during which bombing techniques were developed while he waited for new aircraft and

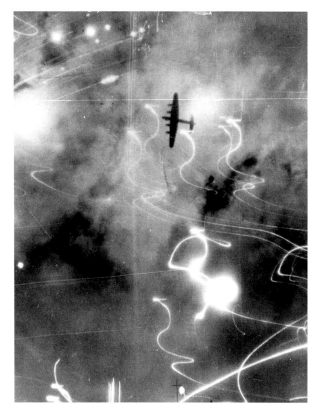

technology with which to prosecute the main offensive. The first few days of 1943 saw the emergence of two new bomber groups, the Pathfinder Force becoming No. 8 (PFF) Group on 8 January and the Canadian units gathered within No. 4 Group becoming No. 6 (RCAF) Group. The latter had actually formed in October 1942, but was declared operational on New Year's Day 1943. Henceforth, the Canadian government paid for its operations.

Apart from the extraordinary Thousand Bomber Raids, attacks by 250 aircraft had represented a 'maximum effort' during 1942. During 1943 a maximum effort would involve 450 bombers. Moreover, from a Command dominated by the Wellington, Harris would have a force dominated by

LEFT An Avro Lancaster of No. 1 Group, Bomber Command, silhouetted against flares, smoke and explosions during the attack on Hamburg, Germany, by aircraft of Nos 1, 5 and 8 Groups on the night of 30/31 January 1943. This raid was the first occasion on which H2S centimetric radar was used by the Pathfinder aircraft to navigate the force to the target. (Photo by British Official Photo/Time & Life)

four-engined bombers and average bomb load per aircraft more than doubled.

Following an experimental Oboe raid on Düsseldorf by Pathfinder Mosquitos and Lancasters on 31 December/1 January, further raids were mounted using PFF Mosquitos with No. 5 Group Lancasters. Three of 19 Lancasters despatched against Essen on 3/4 January and two of 29 sent out against the same target on 4/5 January were lost, but accuracy was good. A follow-up raid on 7/8 January saw all 19 Lancasters return safely, but these caused less damage.

Pathfinder Mosquitos used Oboe to mark for 38 Lancasters that attacked Duisburg without loss on 8/9 January, and for 50 Lancasters attacking Essen the following night, suffering three losses. The Oboe-marked offensive against Essen continued on 11/12 (with one of 72 Lancasters failing to return), 12/13 (one of 55 Lancasters being lost) and 13/14 January (four of 66 Lancasters failed to return). Four of 79 Lancasters were lost when No. 5 Group returned to Essen on 21/22 January, bombing blind through total cloud cover.

October 1942 had seen the introduction of the radial-engined Lancaster B.Mk II, a handful of which were issued to a flight within No. 61 Sqn at Syerston. This small trials unit finally began operations on 11 January 1943.

The year had begun with a major diversion from Harris's strategic offensive. A 14 January directive from the War Cabinet ordered him to mount area attacks against French cities adjacent to U-boat operating bases, singling out Lorient, St Nazaire, Brest and La Pallice (in order of priority). These attacks were quite specifically not against the U-boats themselves, nor even the docks in which they were based, but aimed to devastate maintenance facilities and basic services like power, water and light, and (although this were left unstated) the locally recruited workers who augmented Kriegsmarine personnel.

The essential services were protected by newly built reinforced concrete U-boat pens, or dispersed into the surrounding countryside, however, and the offensive against Lorient and St Nazaire had little effect, except on the French civilian population. Attacks against Brest and La Pallice were abandoned when the results of the raids against the initial targets became clear.

This anti-U-boat campaign began on 14/15 January 1943, with the 122-aircraft force including six Lancasters. Target marking was accurate, but Main Force bombing was described as 'wild'. Four Lancasters were among the 157 aircraft that returned to Lorient on 15/16 January, when bombing was more effective. Lancasters played a relatively minor role in the raids against Lorient, being heavily outnumbered by other types.

However, on 7/8 February, the 323 attackers included 80 Lancasters, which contributed to a devastating attack, although three Avro bombers were lost. Lorient received an even heavier attack on 13/14 February, and 164 Lancasters outnumbered all other types in a raid that saw more than 1,000 tons of bombs dropped for the first time in an unreinforced Main Force attack. Two Lancasters were lost. The final attack against Lorient came on 16/17 February, with 377 bombers being sortied. These included 131

Lancasters, one of which was lost. In eight major raids, Bomber Command dropped 4,000 tons of bombs on the French port, losing 24 aircraft in the process.

On 16/17 January, Bomber Command mounted its first major raid on Berlin since 1941, sending out 190 Lancasters and 11 Halifaxes. The force found Berlin ill-prepared for the attack, with half its *Flak* personnel away on a training course and inadequate air raid warnings leaving the streets full. Despite cloud and haze causing inaccurate bombing, 198 people were killed on the ground and the 10,000-seat Deutschlandehalle (Europe's biggest covered hall) was burned out after being evacuated without casualties. One Lancaster failed to return.

Berlin would never be attacked so cheaply again, as was demonstrated the following night when 19 Lancasters (of 170) and three Halifaxes (of 17) were

OPPOSITE A crew of a Lancaster bomber chalk up an 'all back' message on their return from a major bombing raid against E-Boats at Boulogne, using 5,000lb bombs. (Photo by © Hulton-Deutsch Collection/CORBIS/Corbis via Getty Images)

downed. One of the surviving Lancasters, flown by No. 106 Sqn's CO, Guy Gibson, carried the BBC's Richard Dimbleby.

Lancasters formed the backbone of two attacks against Düsseldorf during January, with 80 aircraft (backed by three Mosquitos) attacking the city on 23/24 January, and 124 (backed by 33 Halifaxes and five Mosquitos) on 27/28 January. The second raid saw the first use of ground markers by the Oboe Mosquitos, backed up by PFF Lancasters. The bombing was concentrated and caused substantial damage.

Lancasters were used in attacks against Hamburg on 30/31 January and 3/4 February. These proved relatively ineffective, despite the Pathfinders using H2S to mark the targets.

In between these raids was an attack on Cologne on 2/3 February using experimental marking techniques, although both H2S and Oboe proved disappointing. Three of the 116 Lancasters sent out were lost. A similar attack on the same target on 14/15 February proved no more successful.

Difficulties with H2S and sky-marking inaccuracy were responsible for bombs falling south of their aiming point in Wilhelmshaven on 11/12 February. However, in falling wide the bombs caused a huge explosion that destroyed the naval ammunition store at Mariensiel, devastating 120 acres and inflicting damage on the dockyard and town. Three of 129 Lancasters failed to return.

The campaign against Italian cities continued with an attack on Turin on 4/5 February. Four No. 8 Group Lancasters mounted a simultaneous raid on La Spezia with 'airburst' 4,000lb blast bombs that exploded 200ft above the ground to maximise blast effect.

On the night of 14/15 February, Sergeant Ivan Hazard of No. 101 Sqn flew one of 142 Lancasters from Nos 1, 5 and 8 Groups that set out to attack Milan. A Fiat CR.42 attacked the bomber over the target, setting it on fire and igniting incendiaries that had failed to release.

This sent flames over the mid-upper turret and

gunner, Sergeant Dove, who stayed at his post to drive off the attacker even as ammunition in the turret began to explode. Despite his burned hands and face, Dove downed the fighter, which had been damaged by the rear gunner. Ignoring his wounds, and the fire burning fiercely in the fuselage, he struggled aft to assist the wounded rear gunner from his turret.

While the rest of the crew tackled the fire, Hazard managed to fly his crippled Lancaster home, gaining sufficient height to re-cross the Alps, despite losing an engine en route. Sergeants Hazard, Dove, Airey (rear gunner), Bain (flight engineer) and Williams (navigator) were all awarded CGMs, while the bomb aimer, Pilot Officer Gates, was awarded a DSO. Two Lancasters failed to return.

Poor marking by the Pathfinders severely limited the effectiveness of a series of February missions flown against Wilhelmshaven, Bremen, Nuremberg and Cologne. The RAF lost 35 bombers, including 17 Lancasters, having mounted more than 1,600 sorties.

Harris's so-called 'Main Offensive' began in the spring of 1943 with what became known as the Battle of the Ruhr. Harris would probably have preferred to strike against Berlin, but realised that a serious offensive against the German capital would have to wait for longer nights, improved bombing and target-marking techniques, and an answer to the menace posed by *Flak* and fighters.

This was proved on 1/2 March, when 17 of the attacking force of 302 aircraft were lost, including seven of 156 Lancasters. Bombing accuracy was good, however, and damage heavy. Most significantly, Bomber Command managed to knock out a Telefunken factory where a captured H2S set (from a Stirling) was being re-assembled. The set was destroyed, but the Germans received a new one the same night from a No. 35 Sqn Halifax that crashed in Holland!

The limitations of H2S were starkly revealed during an attack on Hamburg on 3/4 March, when the Pathfinders mistook mud banks in the Elbe, 14 miles south of the city, for Hamburg docks. The town of Wedel (including a naval clothing store) was hit harder than Hamburg, and ten of the 417 attacking aircraft were downed, including four of 149 Lancasters.

The Ruhr was a better target – more important to the German war economy, closer and thus more accessible to Bomber Command's bases, and with a dense concentration of important targets. But the cities in the Ruhr valley were not easy targets, being heavily defended by belts of searchlights, AA and night-fighter control boxes. The defences were so heavy, in fact, that even at the height of the battle, Bomber Command had to keep hitting other targets, from Stettin to Turin, to discourage the Germans from committing even more resources to the defence of the Ruhr cities.

The number of bombers despatched on raids increased steadily during the Battle, but began with occasional raids by as many as 600. The first raid of the offensive was made against Essen on 5/6 March. Marking was accurate, despite a ground haze, and 442 aircraft (including 157 Lancasters) inflicted heavy damage during a 40-minute attack. Two-thirds of the bombs dropped were incendiaries and of the remainder, one-third was fused for long delays. Stragglers hit six other Ruhr valley cities. Four Lancasters failed to return.

On 8/9 March, Bomber Command ranged further to attack Nuremberg with 335 aircraft. Haze prevented accurate marking, and only half of the bombs dropped hit the city. Nevertheless, damage was heavy. Two of the 170 Lancasters failed to return.

It was Munich's turn the next night, with 264 aircraft (including 142 Lancasters) attacking. Five Lancasters were lost, yet despite local *Flak* firing 14,234 rounds and seven night fighters being active over the target, only one RAF bomber actually fell over Munich itself.

The remainder of March saw a lacklustre raid on Stuttgart on 11/12, a more successful attack on Essen the following night, and further raids against St Nazaire, Duisburg and Berlin.

April was a busy month for Bomber Command, with attacks against Duisburg, Essen, Mannheim, Stuttgart, Frankfurt, Kiel, La Spezia, Pilsen and Stettin.

Results varied, but marking was generally good and damage correspondingly heavy. The initial April attack on Essen was the first occasion on which more than 200 Lancasters participated and the month's raids cost 81 Lancasters in all.

May followed a similar pattern to April, but with larger numbers of aircraft despatched and greater participation by the growing fleet of Lancasters. The month saw major raids against Bochum, Dortmund, Duisburg, Düsseldorf, Essen, Wuppertal and Pilsen. Some 47 Lancasters were lost during these attacks, but damage was heavy on the ground.

'DAMBUSTERS': OPERATION *CHASTISE*

The dams and reservoirs of Germany's industrial heartland had been studied for attack before the war. It was realised by 1938 that dams were difficult targets, requiring a specialised weapon and a suitable method to deliver it.

The Möhne, Sorpe and Eder dams held the majority of water in the Ruhr, and were considered for attack, along with the Ennepe, Lister and Diemel dams. It was decided that the Möhne should take priority, since its destruction would seriously affect hydroelectricity generation and cause massive flooding and destruction in the valley downstream.

Barnes Wallis was assistant chief designer at Vickers-Armstrong Aviation when war broke out in 1939. His initial idea for attacking the dams envisaged a massive bomb dropped from great height, which would destroy them through the shock waves it created underground. The idea resulted in the Tallboy and Grand Slam bombs, but was found unsuitable for an attack on the dams.

Wallis then calculated that charges detonated against the dam wall would weaken it sufficiently to eventually cause a breach. He calculated that 6,000lb of RDX high explosive would be sufficient. But anti-torpedo nets prevented mines or other subsurface weapons reaching the dam walls. Thus, Wallis began his famous garden experiments, where he bounced marbles across the surface of water in a tub.

His bomb was initially spherical in shape, but

tended to break up and weave off its bouncing course. The final design, known as the Upkeep mine, was a more reliable barrel shape.

A special squadron was required for the raid which, due to the limited time available for training, would have to include some of the Command's most experienced crews. The new unit was part of No. 5 Group and its commander, Air Vice Marshal The Honourable Ralph Cochrane chose one of his most experienced leaders, Wing Commander Guy Gibson, to head Squadron 'X', as it was initially known.

Number 617 Squadron subsequently formed at RAF Scampton on 21 March, and crews began transferring in. Lancasters were borrowed for training until the unit's modified 'Provisioning' Lancasters arrived. The

OPPOSITE Wg Cdr G.P. Gibson (centre), with his two Flight Commanders, Sqn Ldr J. H. Searby (left) and Sqn Ldr P. Ward-Hunt, at Syerston, Nottinghamshire in March 1943. Searby took over command of 106 Sqn from Gibson, while Gibson went on to lead the newly-formed No. 617 Sqn at Scampton, Lincolnshire. Behind them stands Gibson's Avro Lancaster B Mark I, ED593/ZN-Y 'Admiral Prune II'. (Photo by IWM via Getty Images)

squadron was ready to go by early May 1943.

Nineteen aircraft flew the Operation *Chastise* mission, divided into three sections. The first section of nine aircraft, led by Gibson, would attack the Möhne and, if successful, move on to the Eder. The second section of five aircraft would attack the Sorpe and the third section of five would act as reserve, briefed to attack 'last resort' targets or the main targets if any had not been breached.

The mission was scheduled for when water levels in the dams were at their highest, and the night of 16 May was chosen. The first wave took off from Scampton at 21:30. After crossing the Rhine, an aircraft in the second section, flown by Flight Lieutenant Bill Astell, was hit by *Flak* from two positions, but flew on for several miles before it was engulfed in flames.

Gibson's section arrived over the Möhne unscathed. He attacked first and hit the target despite intense ground fire, but did not breach the dam. Flight Lieutenant Hopwood attacked second. His aircraft was badly hit during the run and the bomb was released late. The aircraft staggered away from the dam before exploding. Gibson then escorted Flight Lieutenant Martin's attack, drawing away some of the ground fire, but the mine exploded early.

Martin and Gibson then escorted Squadron Leader 'Dinghy' Young, who released perfectly. The mine exploded against the dam, but no breach appeared. The fifth aircraft, flown by Flight Lieutenant David Maltby, attacked and just as its Upkeep released, the dam began to collapse.

Five aircraft had not released their mines and headed to the Eder, led by Gibson, while the others returned home. They arrived to find the dam undefended, although the surrounding hilly terrain demanded not only great piloting skill, but also the Lancaster's full manoeuvrability.

Flight Lieutenant Dave Shannon was first to attack, his weapon causing a slight breach. Next came Squadron Leader Henry Maudslay, whose weapon fell late, hit the dam wall and exploded, catching the Lancaster in its blast. Maudslay's aircraft seemed to disappear, but had survived the blast only to be shot down by *Flak* on the way back to Scampton; none of the crew survived. Last to attack was Pilot Officer Les Knight, whose mine was released perfectly, bouncing to the dam and sinking before exploding. It widened the breach and a great tidal wave swept down the Eder valley.

The second wave had departed after Gibson's. Two of its aircraft were forced back, Flight Lieutenant Les Munro returning after *Flak* damaged his Lancaster, while Pilot Officer Rice returned after his Upkeep mine clipped the sea and was lost. Two other aircraft were not heard from again.

Flight Lieutenant Barlow's aircraft crashed near the German–Dutch border. *Flak* brought Pilot Officer Byers' Lancaster down off the island of Texel on the Dutch

OPPOSITE During the 'Dambusters' raid of 16 May, 1943, after four abortive attempts Flt Lt D. J. Shannon's aircraft releases the Upkeep mine, which exploded against the dam wall. The dam was finally broken by the third aircraft to attack, flown by PO L. G. Knight. (Adam Tooby © Osprey Publishing)

coast, leaving Flight Lieutenant Joe McCarthy to press on alone to the Sorpe. He damaged, but did not breach the dam, before returning safely to Scampton.

The third wave, led by Pilot Officer Bill Ottley, crossed the Rhine, where Ottley's aircraft was hit by *Flak* and exploded. *Flak* shot down the second aircraft, flown by Pilot Officer Burpee, over Gilze-Rijen airfield. The third aircraft, flown by Flight Sergeant Anderson (who took off last), returned to Scampton with its Upkeep mine intact. His rear turret had become unserviceable necessitating large detours to avoid areas of heavy *Flak*, and he had also encountered areas of mist making navigation difficult. As a result Anderson fell behind schedule and with dawn only an hour away, returned to Scampton.

Only two aircraft were left to head to the Sorpe dam. Flight Sergeant Ken Brown hit the dam but did not

OPPOSITE A German photograph of the breached Möhne Dam the day after the raid by No. 617 Sqn. One aircraft and four aircrew were lost during the attack on the Möhne. (Photo by Keystone/Getty Images)

breach it; he returned safely to Scampton. Flight Sergeant Bill Townend attacked the Ennepe dam without success, and with daylight getting close, raced back to Scampton, arriving safely at 06:15, the last to return.

Chastise had been successful and had once again demonstrated the Lancaster's capability, with two of the attack's main targets breached. The squadron's losses were excessive, however. Eight of the 19 Lancasters despatched failed to return and 53 aircrew were killed.

BATTLE OF THE RUHR

June saw the wider Battle of the Ruhr continuing at an accelerating pace. On 11/12, 783 aircraft (including 326 Lancasters and 202 Halifaxes) attacked Düsseldorf. Some 14 Lancasters failed to return, but 1,292 people were killed, 140,000 'bombed out' and heavy destruction achieved. On the same night, 29 Lancasters dominated the 72-aircraft No. 8 Group force that attacked Münster in a mass trial of H2S. Between them, the two attacks represented the largest Bomber Command effort since the Thousand Bomber Raids.

More consistent results were now being achieved and June's attacks on Ruhr towns were generally extremely effective, although they cost 107 Lancasters, fine weather allowing the German night fighters considerable success. June also saw the low-level raid against the Schneider works at Le Creusot and a special mission to the Zeppelin works at Friedrichshafen, on the shores of Lake Constance.

The latter target had been attacked on 20/21 June, 60 No. 5 Group Lancasters being guided by a Master Bomber (Wing Commander G. L. Gomm of No. 467 Sqn taking over from Group Captain Slee after the latter's aircraft developed engine trouble). Due to attack from between 5,000 and 10,000ft, the Lancasters were forced by heavy *Flak* to bomb instead from 15,000ft, where they were hampered by strong winds. The factory was devastated, however, and the raiders flew on to land in North Africa. During their return, on 23/24 June, 52 Lancasters attacked La Spezia.

Number 426 Sqn joined No. 6 (RCAF) Group as a Lancaster unit during June 1943, trading in its Merlin-powered Halifaxes.

The offensive continued in July, with Cologne coming under heavy attack on 3/4 and 8/9 July. The first raid saw the emergence of the Luftwaffe's new *Wilde Sau* (Wild Boar) tactics, in which single-seat fighters used the illumination from searchlights, target markers and burning buildings to attack bombers in the target area. Despite this innovation, the night's loss rate was routine. Bomber Command ventured beyond the Ruhr to Turin on 12/13 July, and the Peugeot works at Montbéliard were hit on 15/16 July.

HAMBURG

Towards the end of July 1943, the Battle of the Ruhr eased off and Bomber Command's attention turned to Hamburg. A ten-day campaign between 24 July and 3 August saw four very heavy and accurate attacks against Germany's second largest city. Hamburg was also the country's largest port and although both the city and port were beyond Oboe range, they were considered ideal targets for H2S.

The first raid on 24 July comprised 791 aircraft, of which 347 were Lancasters. The raid caused considerable damage to the city centre and surrounding districts and introduced a technological landmark; Window had been used for the first time against the *Wurzburg* search radar, causing great confusion among the ground defences.

The force returned to Hamburg three nights later (with 353 Lancasters out of a strength of 787). The dry, hot weather conditions combined with the concentrated bombing to develop a firestorm lasting several hours. A third raid on the night of 30 July (with 340 Lancasters out of a force strength of 777) bombed the remaining areas of the city, causing heavy damage. The last raid, on the night of 2 August, was disrupted by bad weather, and many crews bombed alternative targets.

The Lancaster played a major role in the effort against Hamburg. Almost half the 3,000 sorties launched against it were by Lancasters and the aircraft dropped around 10,000 tons of bombs on the city for the loss of 39 aircraft.

PEENEMÜNDE

Number 7 Sqn re-equipped with Lancasters in July, trading in its aging Stirlings. In advance of the planned invasion of Italy, Bomber Command received orders from the War Cabinet to undertake a brief campaign against Italian cities, with the aim of encouraging an Italian surrender. The first raid, against Genoa, Milan and Turin by 197 Lancasters, saw No. 83 Sqn's Group Captain Searby rehearsing his role as Master Bomber for the up-coming attack against Peenemünde. The Command returned to Italy several times before making its last raid, against Turin, on 16/17 August. Flown by 154 aircraft, the attack included 14 Pathfinder Lancasters. The raids proved pivotal in forcing Italy out of the war.

Bomber Command also continued hitting German cities during August, at a cost of 30 Lancasters. But its most important mission that month was on 17/18 August, when 324 Lancasters, 218 Halifaxes and 54 Stirlings set out against the German rocket research establishment at Peenemünde. The attack was unique, in that the whole Main Force attempted a precision raid against a single target. Searby flew as Master Bomber, and the Pathfinders marked three aiming points in succession as the raid developed – first the scientists' accommodation block, then the rocket factory and finally the experimental facilities.

A diversionary Mosquito attack on Berlin drew off most of the defending night fighters, but 40 bombers (including 23 Lancasters) were lost, about a dozen of them to *Schräge Musik*-equipped night fighters that found the bomber stream on its way home.

The heavy overall casualties were deemed worthwhile, since Peenemünde was hit very hard and the V2 rocket programme put back by several months. Many bomber aircrew were decorated for their actions that night, not least Warrant Officer W. L. Wilson, a No. 467 Sqn pilot who received a DFC, and Sergeant George Oliver (his mid-upper gunner), presented with a CGM.

Wilson's Lancaster was hit by a fighter's cannon fire after bombing Peenemünde, wounding his rear gunner and shooting away the elevator and rudder trim. He evaded further attacks and flew the crippled bomber back to base, while Oliver downed the enemy aircraft and then put out the fires, with the assistance of the rest of the crew.

Two Halifax units converted to Lancasters during August 1943, No. 405 Sqn with No. 8 (PFF) Group and No. 6 (RCAF) Group's No. 408 Sqn.

Following the success of the Peenemünde raid, Harris launched a series of three attacks against Berlin, spread over a 12-night period. Mounted on 23/24

OPPOSITE These photo-reconnaissance images of Peenemünde, taken before and after the 17/18 August 1943 attack on the rocket research establishment, clearly show how effective this raid was. Although the main building remains standing and substantially intact, it has been burned out and part of its roof blown off. (Left: Photo by Keystone-France\Gamma-Rapho via Getty Images and right: © IWM C 4783)

August, 31 August/1 September and 3/4 September, these raids may have been intended to mark the beginning of a full-scale onslaught on the Reich capital, but heavy losses and poor accuracy saw the full Battle of Berlin postponed.

Apart from area attacks on cities, Bomber Command Lancasters also carried out a number of precision raids. Number 617 Sqn despatched eight aircraft with new 12,000lb bombs against the Dortmund–Ems canal on 14/15 September, but these were recalled due to fog in the target area. One aircraft crashed into the sea, killing the pilot (David Maltby, a Dams raid veteran) and his crew. The squadron launched against the same target on 15/16 September, but five aircraft failed to return, including those of another Dams veteran, Australian L. G. Knight, and the new CO, Squadron Leader G. W. Holden.

Bomber Command operations continued to follow much the same pattern, albeit with more gaps due to poor weather, and with cloud causing a minor deterioration in marking accuracy. On 3 November, Flight Lieutenant Bill Reid of No. 61 Sqn earned himself a Victoria Cross after pressing on to Dusseldorf when he would have been justified in returning to base. An initial night-fighter attack wiped out his rear turret and wounded Reid in the head, shoulder and hands. A second attack killed the navigator and mortally wounded the wireless operator, while the mid-upper turret, elevator trim tabs, intercom and oxygen system were knocked out.

Reid's flight engineer, Sergeant James Norris, was awarded a CGM for his efforts in assisting the wounded Reid to the target, and for then taking over and flying the aircraft back home, not mentioning his own wounds until after Reid had landed the aircraft at the USAAF base at Shipdham.

The extent of damage to property and industry was becoming almost incredible. On several occasions during the year, Bomber Command virtually destroyed entire cities as working entities, most notably with the

OPPOSITE Crew loading a 400lb 'Cookie' bomb onto a Lancaster bomber, around 1940. (Photo by Hulton Archive/Getty Images)

firestorms at Hamburg, but also at Kassel and Frankfurt. It had also begun what was to become its most difficult and dangerous struggle – the assault on Berlin.

BATTLE OF BERLIN

The Battle of Berlin began in earnest on the night of 18/19 November 1943, and Bomber Command had mounted eight additional raids against the German capital by month-end. Four more followed in December and the battle continued to its zenith in 1944.

Harris continued to believe that Germany could be defeated through bombing alone, and set his sights on reducing the German capital to rubble. 'We can wreck Berlin from end to end if the USAAF will come in on it. It will cost us between 400 and 500 aircraft. It will cost Germany the war,' Harris told Churchill, and in a letter to the Air Ministry on 7 December 1943, he claimed he could destroy Berlin, and bring the war to an end, by 1 April 1944.

Harris described the aim of his attacks on Berlin as being 'to cause the heart of the German nation to stop beating', and felt disinclined to apologise for directly targeting the enemy civilian population. When pressed to use a higher proportion of incendiaries, he argued the case for High Explosives (HE), saying:

> I do not agree with this policy. The morale effect of HE is vast. People can escape from fires, and the casualties on a solely fire raising raid would be as nothing. What we want to do in addition to the horrors of fire is to bring the masonry crashing down on top of the Boche, to kill the Boche and to terrify the Boche.

Berlin was an undeniably attractive target. Of enormous symbolic value as the capital of the Reich, Berlin also housed the inner workings of the Nazi machinery of government and all of the vital ministries that ran the German war effort. Berlin was also a hugely important industrial centre, with a number of tank, aircraft engine, instrument and machine tool factories and one quarter of Germany's electrical engineering industry. It was also a vitally important communications hub between the Western and Eastern Fronts, and was the third largest city in the world, making it an ideal morale target.

Had Bomber Command been able to wreak the same level of destruction upon Berlin as it had on Hamburg, some historians believe that Harris could have brought the war to an early end. But Berlin was not Hamburg, and it was never likely that Bomber Command would be able to hit it anything like so hard, or to such devastating effect.

Berlin was 150 miles further inside Germany and well inland. It thus demanded an overland approach through miles of hostile and heavily defended airspace, well beyond the range of Oboe. Berlin was also a poor target for H2S, stretching Bomber Command's navigational capabilities to the limit, even after the introduction of Gee-H in November 1943.

The city was also far enough from Bomber Command's bases to force uneasy compromises for the Lancaster squadrons, with a need to balance bomb load, performance, range and armour. It was also a massive, sprawling city, whose important targets could easily be missed without accurate marking and it was very heavily defended.

Moreover, Hamburg had been attacked in summer, before missions began to be affected by cloud cover over the target, and before the German night-fighter arm had really developed adequate counters to the latest advances in Bomber Command's technology and equipment.

By the time Bomber Command embarked on its campaign against Berlin, taking advantage of longer winter nights, the weather was often poor and defences had improved. The new SN-2 *Lichtenstein* radar was in widespread service, and German night-fighter crews and their controllers had developed and refined new *Zähme Sau* (Tame Boar) tactics, using radar-equipped night fighters in a more flexible and autonomous fashion where they were vectored to the bomber stream and then found and engaged their own targets.

By February 1944, the Luftwaffe had deployed 200 SN-2 sets (which were better able to differentiate between real targets and Window), and most of these were available for the later stages of the Battle of Berlin. The Germans also made even greater use of searchlights and used high-flying Junkers Ju 88s to drop parachute flares above the bomber stream.

Worse still, the Luftwaffe had discovered Bomber Command's Monica tail warning radar, and H2S had also been compromised. It was a relatively easy matter to develop and deploy the *Flensburg* homer (which enabled a night-fighter pilot to home onto a Monica-equipped bomber) and the *Naxos-Z*, which could detect and locate H2S emissions.

Only 28 enemy fighters were equipped with *Naxos-Z*, but there were also ground-based systems that could detect and roughly locate H2S, while the way in which it was used also imposed vulnerabilities. This was because aircraft without H2S often flew decoy raids, while the real attackers used H2S intensively for route navigation and target finding. This sometimes allowed German controllers to ignore spoof raids and concentrate their efforts on the vulnerable Main Force bombers. These new devices effectively turned Monica and H2S into homing beacons for enemy fighters, while there was also equipment that could detect a bomber's IFF (identification friend or foe) transmissions.

An increasing number of night fighters were also equipped with upward-firing 20mm or 30mm cannon (known as *Schräge Musik* – literally sloping music – or jazz). These enabled a night fighter to fly underneath a bomber (in its blind spot) and pour a concentrated stream of fire into its belly, bomb bay and fuel tanks. Only the handful of bombers equipped with FN64 ventral turrets or improvised belly machine guns had any counter to this devastating weapon.

But the bomber war was always a shifting pattern of measure and countermeasure, and the Battle of Berlin saw the RAF make its first use of a number of new devices intended to disrupt night-fighter operations. During the Battle of Berlin, arguably the most important of these countermeasures was Airborne Cigar (ABC) and some No. 101 Sqn Main Force Lancasters carried it from October.

It comprised a high-powered VHF jammer, targeted against the German 38-42MHz FuG 16ZY radio used to transmit a running commentary of the bomber stream's position, course and altitude. ABC also jammed the night fighters' *Benito* navigation aid and was eventually fitted to Fortresses and Halifaxes with the RAF's dedicated Bomber Support organisation, No. 100 Group, although it was not officially formed until 23 November 1943, too late for the Battle of Berlin.

Number 101 Sqn's ABC Lancasters usually flew with a full bomb load, yet carried three separate jammers and a Special Duties Operator. This German linguist found enemy transmissions, listened to them to ascertain whether they were fighter control frequencies and then tuned his jammers into them, suppressing the signal to see whether new frequencies were being used and, if necessary, jamming those too.

OPPOSITE A Lancaster bombing the Pauillac oil store and refinery at D'Ambes on 4 August 1944. (Cody Images)

Because No. 101 Sqn's ABC-equipped Lancasters accompanied every Main Force raid, the squadron expanded to meet its heavy commitments, with 36 and later 42 aircraft – plus four reserves. Bombers also used Mandrel to jam German *Freya* early warning radar, and Tinsel to broadcast engine noise over fighter control frequencies. The squadron frequently despatched 30 aircraft in a single night, and (because their transmissions could be detected by enemy fighters) suffered heavy casualties – it lost 21 aircraft and 168 aircrew during the first ten weeks of the Battle of Berlin.

The bombers could also count on limited fighter support, at least until the end of 1943, with Serrate-equipped Mosquitos and Beaufighters using their equipment to home onto the air intercept radar carried by enemy night fighters, and with other Mosquitos flying Flower missions – attacks against enemy night-fighter airfields as the enemy aircraft took off and the bomber stream crossed the coast. Other radar-equipped Mosquitos flew Mahmoud patrols, flying straight and level to simulate a stray bomber, then using Monica to detect an approaching enemy night fighter before turning to get onto the enemy aircraft's tail.

The fighters enjoyed considerable success, but there were too few to do more than complicate the lives of the enemy crews, demoralising some and perhaps causing a higher accident rate as they flew at lower level while preparing to land. But the *Nachtjagdwaffe* (night-fighter force) was at the peak of its powers, with the best equipment it had ever had.

Another enemy faced by the bomber crews was the winter weather, which made life more uncomfortable and navigation more difficult. Even if an aircraft fought its way to and from the target unscathed, the weather could be deadly. The low-lying bomber airfields in East Anglia, Lincolnshire and Yorkshire were often affected by fog, and aircraft (especially damaged ones) frequently came to grief in these conditions.

The winter of 1943 saw the introduction of the Fog Investigation and Dispersal Operation (FIDO) system at 15 (mainly Bomber Command) bases. FIDO fed fuel under pressure along pipes beside the main runway,

where it was vaporised and burned to thermally disperse convection fog. The result was a clear 'tunnel' in which aircraft could land.

The Wellington flew its last raid on 8/9 October 1943, just before the Battle of Berlin, as an increasing proportion of the bomber force was equipped with the Lancaster, including a number of new units flying radial-engined B.Mk IIs. Among these, the RAF's Nos 61, 115 and 426 Sqns were joined by two RCAF units, Nos 408 and 432 Sqns, which converted in August and September, and No. 514 Sqn, RAF.

The aircraft's relatively poor ceiling led aircrew to make unfavourable comparisons to the Lancaster B.Mk I, but it was a superb replacement for Wellingtons or Stirlings. Moreover, its air-cooled radial engines were much less vulnerable to battle damage, and, as a

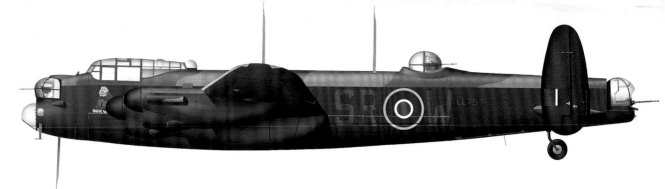

ABOVE Lancaster B.Mk I LL757/SR-W 'Oor Wullie' was with No. 101 Sqn at Ludford Magna in July 1944. Typical of the unit's ABC-equipped Lancasters, it sprouted antennas for its high-powered transmitters, and quickly gained a Rose tail turret housing a pair of 0.50in machine guns. No. 101 Sqn began using the Rose turret in May 1944, prior to it being officially cleared for service in September. This aircraft was the regular mount of PO Waughman and his crew until it failed to return from an operation to Stettin on 30 August 1944. Flt Lt W. A. M. B. Stewart and his nine-man crew were posted missing. (Chris Davey © Osprey Publishing)

further bonus, the type enjoyed far better ditching characteristics.

Crucially, at least insofar as its crews were concerned, the B.Mk II was also superior to the Merlin-engined version in almost every other area of performance, as No. 432 Sqn's Flying Officer Jim McIntosh remembered:

These things went like skinned cats! I bet we could outrun the fighters. We had to concede to the Is and IIIs a bit on the bombing altitude, but on anything else we were better. Faster, quicker off the deck, less exhaust glow at night, no glycol and less engine trouble.

Most B.Mk IIs were fitted with bulged bomb doors allowing carriage of an 8,000lb weapon. Moreover, early suggestions that the aircraft might be used for day bombing had led to provision for an FN64 ventral turret, manned by an eighth crew member. Some squadron commanders retained the turret while others had it removed. The B.Mk II could not carry H2S bombing radar and so pioneered the use of Gee-H. This proved extremely effective during early operations, but lacked the range to be useful against Berlin and was removed from Main Force aircraft pending a return to shorter-range operations.

The Mk IIs were heavily used during the Battle of Berlin, but with production of the type ending in March 1944, there were insufficient aircraft to replace losses, and the type began disappearing from the front line. Number 432 Sqn converted to the Halifax III in February 1944 and No. 115 followed between March and May.

Although known as the Battle of Berlin, the period covering the winter of 1943–44 also saw Bomber Command attacking other targets. Had Harris attempted to strike Berlin every time the weather permitted, losses would have reduced Bomber Command to no more than a cadre within days.

Also, by dividing his attacks between Berlin and other targets Harris made it impossible for the Luftwaffe to concentrate its night fighters in defence of Berlin, giving his bombers some element of surprise. Nonetheless, Berlin suffered its last major attack of the war on 24/25 March 1944. It involved 811 aircraft (577 Lancasters, 216 Halifaxes and 18 Mosquitos), but a powerful wind blew the bomber stream south and played havoc with the PFF's ability to mark the target, so that the main concentration of bombs fell in the south-western districts. Some 44 Lancasters and 28 Halifaxes failed to return.

The Battle of Berlin had failed to bring about the collapse Harris predicted, but many lessons had been learned that would improve Bomber Command's effectiveness. Improved navigational accuracy and the withdrawal of older, slower types enabled a compressed bomber stream, covering a 70-mile strip instead of the 300 miles common in 1942. This meant that 800 aircraft could 'feed through' the target in only about 20 minutes, minimising their exposure to enemy defences.

Many of the Halifaxes and Stirlings dropped from Main Force raids were used to mount massive diversionary operations, using prodigious quantities of Window to simulate a Main Force attack, but actually attacking coastal targets or minelaying.

Almost 400 Bomber Command aircraft were lost in direct raids against Berlin itself, and more were downed in diversionary raids and other attacks mounted during the period.

Harris had conceived his all-out assault on Berlin as including the US Eighth Air Force, operating under his command, by night, in a fully integrated campaign, although such participation was impossible. The USAAF was not about to let its premier combat unit in Europe come under 'foreign' command, even temporarily, while even had it been willing to do so, its crews were not trained for night bombing.

D-DAY AND BEYOND

Harris had stubbornly refused to permit 'his' heavy bombers being diverted to help Coastal Command, undoubtedly giving Germany respite when it most needed it, and when the area bombing campaign was at its least effective and most costly. But eventually, especially after D-Day, he allowed Bomber Command to be used against U-boat pens, harbours and enemy warships with a high degree of success.

Even more surprisingly, Harris threw himself into providing air support for the continental land campaign with some energy and enthusiasm, supporting the invasion itself, and providing close air support and battlefield air interdiction for various ground offensives throughout the rest of the war.

Bomber Command's accuracy continued to improve and it was inevitable that its aircraft would be placed under General Dwight Eisenhower's command to operate in support of Operation *Overlord*, the Allied invasion of occupied Europe in June 1944. Bomber Command was therefore soon tasked with attacking a range of tactical targets in France.

Although there were no traditional all-out area attacks on German cities between 27/28 April (when

Bomber Command attacked Friedrichshafen) and 23/24 July (when Kiel was bombed), raids were flown against German cities containing oil refineries and important railway yards.

Invasion preparations had begun in earnest even as Bomber Command was fighting the Battle of Berlin. French railway targets at Amiens, Laon, Aulnoye, Courtrai and Vaires, along with other industrial targets, were attacked even before the ill-fated Nuremberg raid.

Bomber Command's effort was officially transferred to pre-invasion targets on 14 April 1944. The pace of attacks against railway targets in western Germany, Belgium and France rapidly picked up as the Allies attempted to cut off enemy forces in Normandy from reinforcement by rail. Military camps, armament dumps, depots and factories also came under increasingly heavy attack. A similar level of effort was employed to cut off the Pas de Calais from its reinforcements and supplies in furtherance of the deception that this latter area would actually be the site of the landings.

The campaign against invasion targets saw a further improvement in techniques and targeting accuracy, with an increase in the use of the Mosquito for target marking by Nos 5 and 8 Groups. The former soon began operating as an autonomous force once it had regained Nos 97 and 83 Sqns from the Pathfinders, and also its own Mosquito unit, No. 627 Sqn, while No. 617 gained a sizeable Mosquito flight specifically for target marking duties.

Number 617 Sqn's charismatic CO, Wing Commander Leonard Cheshire, pioneered the technique on 5/6 April 1944 during an attack on an aircraft factory at Toulouse. The Mosquito's high speed and agility gave him the chance to fly three passes over the target at low level before dropping his markers, which were augmented by markers dropped from a pair of No. 617 Sqn Lancasters. The 'ordinary' No. 5 Group Lancaster squadrons then bombed the target so successfully that the technique was immediately adopted.

By the time Bomber Command turned its attention to targets in France, the Lancaster was its primary type, with 40 squadrons on charge, most of them flying B.Mk I/IIIs. The B.Mk II remained, however, and No. 408 Sqn's aircraft flew a highly successful attack against coastal gun emplacements at Longues on D-Day morning, 6 June. Low loss rates allowed the two remaining Lancaster B.Mk II units to serve on into the late summer of 1944, No. 514 trading its aircraft for B.Mk I/IIIs between June and the end of September, while No. 408 completed conversion to the Halifax B.Mk III in August.

Attacks on coastal gun positions began during early May, while in the week leading up to the invasion the bombers attacked German radio listening stations, radar installations and radar jamming facilities, and dropped arms and equipment to the Resistance.

On the night before D-Day, Bomber Command flew a record 1,211 sorties, almost all in direct support of Operation *Overlord*, attacking enemy troops, gun positions, ammunition and oil dumps, and road and rail communications. Enemy E-boats and other light offensive craft were bombed in their French ports.

With the troops ashore, the bombers flew close air support missions, attacking enemy positions within a few hundred yards of friendly soldiers.

Even in the aftermath of the invasion, Bomber Command maintained relentless pressure on German oil targets (especially in the Ruhr), and was diverted into a major offensive against the V1 flying bomb launch sites. Day bombing raids began again after D-Day, but since these were always within range of Allied escort fighters, losses were manageable.

A PRECISION BOMBER

Development of a new 12,000lb HC bomb for special purposes had given No. 617 Sqn a reprieve a year earlier, since it might otherwise have been disbanded following Operation *Chastise*.

The unit's new CO, Squadron Leader G. W. Holden, was told of its planned role as a specialised heavy attack squadron, employing the new 12,000lb HC bomb, initially against the vital Dortmund–Ems canal, which carried raw materials and manufactured goods

between the Ruhr and Germany's northern ports. An abortive attempt on 14/15 September 1943 turned back over the North Sea and a raid was flown without damage the next night. The following night, the new acting CO, Squadron Leader Mickey Martin, led an unsuccessful attack against the Antheor viaduct in the south of France.

Rested, retrained and equipped with a new gyro-stabilised bombsight – the Stabilised Automatic Bomb Sight (SABS) – the squadron soon began achieving average bombing errors of less than 100 yards from 20,000ft. It employed SABS and the 12,000lb HC bomb to re-attack the Antheor viaduct on 11/12 November, but was unable to collapse it, despite three very near misses. Under the command of another new CO, Wing Commander Leonard Cheshire, No. 617 Sqn attacked a number of V1 sites using its new bombs and bombsights on 16/17 and 30/31 December. On 8/9 February, the same weapon was used against the Gnome-Rhône engine plant at Limoges, demolishing the factory.

On 12 February, No. 617 made another attempt against the Antheor viaduct, again failing to destroy it, although a number of attacks against French aircraft and explosives factories using the 12,000lb HC bomb during March proved more successful, and a raid on the railway yards at Juvisy, near Paris, was spectacular.

But the bomb was a primitive device and there was clearly a need for a more accurate heavy weapon that might also penetrate deeply before exploding, enabling it to 'shake' large structures to pieces. Barnes Wallis designed and developed two such weapons in parallel, the 12,000lb Tallboy and 22,000lb Grand Slam. Their tail units imparted a gentle spin as they fell, preventing them from toppling as they reached compressibility. This was routine, since both weapons could attain a terminal velocity of 2,500mph.

Tallboy was first used in anger on 9 June 1944 when No. 617 Sqn dropped 19 devices on the French railway tunnel at Saumur. Constructed within a hill and previously considered virtually impregnable, it was expected to be on the route used to send a Panzer division from southern France to reinforce the Normandy front (the unit had entrained on 8 June).

Cheshire marked the target at one end in a Mosquito, and two more 'Mossies' did the same at the other end, before four No. 83 Sqn Lancasters illuminated the area. The Tallboys were dropped from 10,000ft and several left craters 70ft deep and 100ft wide. One penetrated through to the tunnel, exploding and causing a major collapse.

The squadron successfully used Tallboys against the E-boat pens at Le Havre on 14 June and Boulogne the following day.

Once Germany started launching V1 flying bombs from rapidly erectable pre-fabricated ramps, it became

OPPOSITE Operation *Paravane*: the attack on the German battleship *Tirpitz* moored in Kaa Fjord, Norway on 15 September 1944 . Here, a Lancaster flies towards the target (arrowed, upper left) as a colossal smoke screen is belatedly released by the German defenders. The *Tirpitz* was damaged by one hit and several near misses with Tallboys and was subsequently moved to an anchorage further south in Norway. (Photo by No. 5 Group RAF/ IWM via Getty Images)

doubly necessary to destroy them while they were still in their storage sites. They were stockpiled in underground concrete shelters, which were perfect Tallboy targets, and No. 617 was tasked with attacking the suspected sites at Mimoyecques, Nucourt, Watten and Wizernes.

It also turned its attention to *Tirpitz*, moored in a succession of Norwegian fjords. The long distance between the UK and its Altenfjord mooring ruled out a conventional 'out and return' op, and the decision was taken to fly the mission (Operation *Paravane*) from the USSR, with the attacking aircraft returning to the Soviet base before flying home. The force consisted of 20 SABS-equipped Lancasters from No. 617 Sqn, 18 Lancasters from No. 9 Sqn with conventional Mk XIV bombsights, a photographic Lancaster from No. 463 Sqn, a PRU Mosquito and two Liberators carrying spares and groundcrew. The 11 September journey out was sufficiently difficult for six Lancasters to be written off, while another returned to Britain.

Bad weather delayed the attack until 15 September, when 28 Lancasters set off, only to find an intense smoke screen masking Altenfjord. Seventeen aircraft dropped Tallboys, the others returning to Yagodnik with their Tallboys or 'Johnny Walker' mines still aboard.

Unknown to the RAF, a Tallboy had hit the vessel's bow, creating major damage and causing *Tirpitz* to ship 1,500 tons of water, while other near misses added further damage. The German Navy reluctantly concluded that the vessel's sea-going days were over. It was decided to make minimal repairs and convert it into a floating coastal defence battery.

Tirpitz slipped away, reappearing at Tromsö, 200 miles closer to Scotland, for repairs, before being moored off Haaköy island. Now it was possible to launch a second attack from Scotland, although the Lancasters had to be fitted with auxiliary fuel tanks taken from Wellingtons and Mosquitos. These made them two tons heavier than their normal weight limit, so they were stripped of their front turrets and other equipment, and fitted with more powerful Merlin 24 engines.

On 23/24 September, No. 617 Sqn led a No. 5 Group attack on the Dortmund–Ems canal, which at

last achieved a major breach after two direct hits with Tallboys, although 14 of the 136 attacking Lancasters were lost. The squadron returned to 'dambusting' on 7 October, targeting the floodgates of the Kembs Barrage. One Lancaster bombed from low level, embedding its delay-fused Tallboy in the dam's floodgates. The weapon exploded to create a torrent of water – boats were swept away, some finally 'beaching' in nearby Switzerland.

Numbers 9 and 617 Sqns deployed forward to RAF Lossiemouth on 28 October, and at 0100hrs on 29 October, 20 from each squadron took off to attack *Tirpitz* at Tromsö. They found the fjord shrouded in

LEFT: *Catechism* took place on 12 November 1944. At 0325hrs 29 Lancasters of Nos 617 and 9 squadrons took off from Scotland, once again carrying Tallboy bombs, and set course for Tromsø. No. 617 Sqn attacked first. The first bomb was dropped at 0841hrs, and the last at 0844hrs, followed within seconds by all ten of No. 9 Sqn's Tallboys. The *Tirpitz* appears to have been hit numerous times and damaged by a number of near misses. The ship began to list and then rolled over. (Adam Tooby © Osprey Publishing)

mist and 32 Tallboys were dropped blind, all falling well wide. One aircraft was lost, force landing in Sweden.

On 12 November, 18 No. 617 Sqn Lancasters and 13 from No. 9 attacked again. *Tirpitz* was hit by at least three Tallboys, rolling over soon afterwards. It remained afloat, but upside down.

The squadrons used Tallboys against the U-boat pens at Bergen on 12 January 1945, while No. 617 struck similar installations at Poortershaven on 3 February and No. 9 Sqn used them to attack Ijmuiden, which No. 617 revisited on the 8th.

Among other targets, Nos 9 and 617 Sqns attacked the Bielefeld viaduct with Tallboys several times, but without success. Marshy ground around the viaduct dramatically reduced the Tallboy's effectiveness and it became clear that the structure needed to be attacked using the Grand Slam.

By early 1945 the larger weapon was ready for use, along with a batch of Lancaster B.Mk I (Special) aircraft modified to carry it. Two were delivered to No. 617 Sqn on 13 March and the following day a single Grand Slam destroyed two of the Bielefeld viaduct's pylons and spans, while Tallboys destroyed more. The next Grand Slam target was the Arnsberg viaduct, which carried the main railway line from the Ruhr to Kassel, and was located midway between the Möhne and Sorpe dams. It finally succumbed to five Grand Slams and 13 Tallboys on 19 March.

The Nienburg bridge fell to a Grand Slam and Tallboys on 22 March, before two Grand Slams and two Tallboys destroyed the railway bridge at Bremen. On 27 March, 18 No. 617 Sqn Lancasters (12 armed with the Grand Slam and six with the Tallboy) led 100 Main Force bombers to the U-boat pens at Farge. Two Grand Slams brought down much of the roof and the other bombs rendered the remaining structure unsafe.

Two abortive attempts were made to bomb the pocket battleship *Lutzow* at Swinemünde on 13 and

15 April, before a successful mission on the 16. A near miss tore open the ship's hull and it sank in shallow water. One aircraft was lost, and intense *Flak* damaged all but two of the 18 bombers.

The attack on Berchtesgaden on 25 April, when No. 617 Sqn dropped 16 Tallboys on the SS barracks, was its final strike of the war.

BACK TO GERMANY

Control of Bomber Command's heavies had reverted to the Air Staff on 14 September 1944, although they were almost immediately committed to further tactical work, supporting Operation *Market-Garden*. Tactical operations also continued in France, where 370 Lancasters and 351 Halifaxes attacked Boulogne on 17 September, in preparation for a ground push. The Command then turned its weight on Calais.

Some Allied leaders, including Harris, favoured a return to the general bombing of German cities in an effort to deflate the morale of the German industrial work force. But this was a minority view. Chief of the Air Staff Sir Charles Portal and most of the Air Ministry preferred to concentrate on the German oil and synthetic oil industry, which, they felt, would rob the Wehrmacht of its mobility and effectively ground the Luftwaffe. Eisenhower's air commander (and second in command), Air Chief Marshal Sir Arthur Tedder, favoured continued interdiction of German communications and transport facilities, impressed by Bomber Command's extraordinary contribution to victory in Normandy.

Harris viewed both these as 'panacea targets'. Ordered on 1 November 1944 to 'maintain and if possible intensify' pressure on the 'enemy petroleum industry and oil supplies', and to attack its transport system, he responded unwillingly, finding every possible excuse

ABOVE The Bielefeld viaduct after being attacked by No. 617 Sqn, which dropped a Grand Slam and several Tallboys on the structure on 14 March 1945. The Tallboys left the large craters, while the Grand Slam made a smaller hole (next to the standing pillar in the gap in the viaduct), but penetrated deeply to explode underground. (IWM © C 5086)

(usually weather) to continue with his own strategy, and camouflaging area attacks on cities by nominally aiming at oil or transport targets within them.

The task facing Bomber Command became progressively easier, however, and its losses plummeted – one year after the Battle of Berlin, in October 1944, Bomber Command's loss rate had fallen to less than one per cent. It also had 51 Lancaster squadrons by the end of 1944, and 57 by VE-Day.

Number 3 Group, whose aircraft were now almost fully equipped with Gee-H, was usually able to operate autonomously, like No. 5 Group, leaving Nos 1, 4, 6 and 8 Groups as the Main Force, except when a maximum effort was required.

The final months of the conflict also saw Bomber Command mount some of its largest and heaviest attacks, with raids involving more than 700 Lancasters. It destroyed a number of cities that had previously defied its efforts, and attacked several smaller, less industrialised towns.

Meanwhile, tactics continued to develop and the attack on Brunswick on 12/13 August 1944 was an experimental mission made without Pathfinder support and relying entirely on H2S carried by Main Force aircraft. The 27 August raid on Homberg was Bomber Command's first major daylight attack on Germany since August 1941. Nine Spitfire squadrons escorted the bombers outbound and seven on the withdrawal, and no heavies were lost.

Some attacks were extremely severe, the raid on Darmstadt on 11/12 September killing a reported 8,433 people (and possibly as many as 12,000), and effectively destroying the city in a firestorm.

The raid against Neuss on 23/24 September was the

OPPOSITE Lancaster B.Mk III ND911/V-JN from No. 75 'New Zealand' Sqn, flown by PO Patrick L. McCartin, is illuminated by the a burning Cologne on the night of 31 October 1944. The bomber is being stalked by a Bf 110G-4 night-fighter from IV./NJG 1, its pilot attempting to set up a *Schräge Musik* attack. McCartin managed to avoid the attack, but his luck ran out three weeks later when ND911 was shot down by flak over Homberg. (Gareth Hector, with thanks to Piotr Forkasiewicz for the use of his Lancaster model © Osprey Publishing)

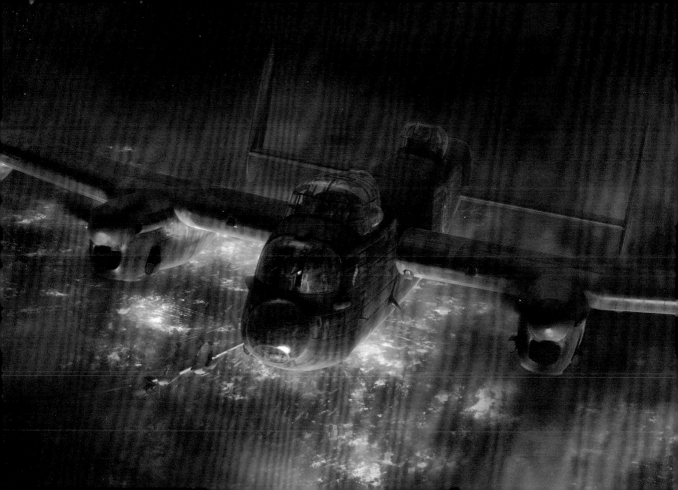

B.Mk II's last, two No. 514 Sqn aircraft participating. Ironically, with the improved tactical situation over Germany, the need for the Lancaster to fly at its maximum height had disappeared, and the B.Mk II, with its less vulnerable air-cooled radial engines and improved performance at lower altitudes, was in many respects a better aircraft for the job.

OPERATION *HURRICANE*

The attack on Dortmund on 6/7 October represented No. 6 (RCAF) Group's largest effort of the war, with 45 Lancasters and 248 Halifaxes. It began what came to be known as the Second Battle of the Ruhr, including Operation *Hurricane*, which began on 14 October and saw the USAAF and Bomber Command attacking targets around the clock. The directive launching the operation dictated:

> In order to demonstrate to the enemy the overwhelming superiority of the Allied Air Forces in this theatre, the intention is to apply within the shortest practical period the maximum effort of the Royal Air Force Bomber Command and the VIII US Bomber Command against objectives in the densely populated Ruhr.

Some 519 Lancasters, 474 Halifaxes and 20 Mosquitos dropped 3,574 tons of HE and 820 tons of incendiaries on Duisberg, with 13 Lancasters and one Halifax falling victim to *Flak*. The USAAF despatched 1,251 further bombers that day, before Bomber Command sent out another 498 Lancasters and 468 Halifaxes (with 39 Mosquitos) in two waves that night (14/15 October), dropping another 4,040 tons of HE and 500 tons of incendiaries. On the same night, No. 5 Group sortied 233 Lancasters against Brunswick.

Number 3 Group's attack on Bonn on 18 October was its first fully independent operation. About a third of the group's Lancasters were equipped with Gee-H and wore colours on their fins. Non Gee-H aircraft were expected to find and formate on a Gee-H machine in the target area and bomb when the Gee-H Lancaster did.

Bonn, previously unbombed, was targeted in this

way so that post-strike reconnaissance would give an accurate impression of the damage caused. The tactic proved devastatingly effective, tearing the heart out of the old city and burning its most historic buildings and university.

On 16 November, Bomber Command briefly returned to a more tactical role. In the area between Aachen and the Rhine, the US First and Ninth Armies were about to attack, and Bomber Command was tasked with striking three towns just behind the lines. It despatched 1,188 aircraft, with 485 Lancasters bombing Düren, 78 bombing Jülich (along with 413 Halifaxes) and 182 No. 3 Group aircraft attacking Heinsberg. The towns were destroyed, but the US advance was bogged down and proved costly.

Intensive attacks continued during November, and during the month No. 150 Sqn joined No. 1 Group at Hemswell, further swelling the Lancaster force. A sharp deterioration in the weather led to a reduction in daylight attacks during December, although some missions were flown after the German army launched its offensive in the Ardennes on the 16.

December saw the first attack against an oil target in eastern Germany. Leuna (targeted on 6/7) was 250 miles from Germany's western border, and 500 miles from Bomber Command's British bases.

These final missions of 1944 saw many examples of quiet heroism, the majority of which usually went unremarked. But on 23 December 1944, 110-mission veteran Squadron Leader Robert Anthony Maurice Palmer DFC of No. 109 Sqn forsook his Mosquito for a No. 582 Sqn Gee-H Lancaster, in which he led 27 Lancasters in an attack against Cologne's marshalling yards.

Palmer's aircraft was badly hit by *Flak* during the run-in to the target, and two engines and the cockpit were set ablaze, but he dropped his bombs on target – the rest of the formation dropping on his signal as was routine during Gee-H attacks. His aircraft then spun in, killing all aboard, but winning the courageous pilot a posthumous VC.

New Year 1945 opened with another VC-winning

act by a Lancaster crewman. During an attack against the Dortmund–Ems canal, No. 9 Sqn wireless operator Flight Sergeant George Thompson went to the aid of his mid-upper gunner, unconscious in a burning turret, dragging him clear despite the fire and exploding ammunition. Having beaten out the flames, suffering severe burns in the process, Thompson rescued the tail gunner, braving the flames again.

Suffering frostbite as he fought his way back to the cockpit to report to the captain, Thompson was so badly injured that the pilot initially failed to recognise him. The wireless op then looked after his comrades until the aircraft made a successful crash landing. He died of his injuries three weeks later.

On 2/3 January Bomber Command destroyed much of Nuremberg, and on 4/5 January, 347 Lancasters attacked Royan, where they killed large numbers of French civilians. The town was held by a particularly stubborn German garrison, which prevented Allied use of the port of Bordeaux. Besieged by Resistance forces, the town held out, and when it was suggested that only Germans and collaborators remained there, it was decided to bomb Royan into submission. But the suggestion was erroneous; Bomber Command had received poor intelligence from Supreme Headquarters Allied Expeditionary Force (SHAEF).

Bomber Command again returned briefly to tactical operations on 7/8 February 1945, sending 156 Lancasters and 292 Halifaxes against the town of Goch and 295 Lancasters against Kleve. The bombers attacked from below cloud, helping clear the way for an attack by the British XXX Corps. The raid was stopped when thick smoke obscured the target, but caused the damage blocked the British advance through Kleve.

Even after the destruction of the most important targets and cities, Bomber Command's attacks continued unabated. There was an understandable desire to do everything possible to erode the defences that stood in the way of the Allied advance, and

OPPOSITE Avro Lancasters of RAF Bomber Command on a daylight raid over the Normandy battlefront, August 1944. (© IWM C 4552)

thereby to 'get it over with' as quickly as possible.

A number of smaller cities and larger towns had not been attacked before 1944. These were often communications hubs, whose destruction was intended to complicate the Wehrmacht's task in deploying reinforcements to the front by causing a massive refugee problem, as well as by destroying key parts of Germany's transport infrastructure. They were often little more than country towns with the misfortune to straddle a vital crossroads, large road or railway.

Bomber Command's Lancaster force continued to expand, as No. 6 Group converted from the Halifax; Nos 424 and 433 Sqns converted during January.

OPERATION *THUNDERCLAP*

Churchill remained keen to do what he could to assist Stalin, and insisted that Bomber Command extend its operations to eastern cities in the path of the Red Army advance, or through which German reinforcements might flow to the Eastern Front. Bomber Command therefore gained a raft of new targets.

The most obvious of these was Dresden, whose destruction has tarnished Bomber Command's reputation and even been cited as an Allied 'war crime'. Under Operation *Thunderclap*, Bomber Command was told to make heavy attacks on Dresden, Chemnitz and Leipzig.

The operation was expected to begin with a raid on Dresden by USAAF day bombers, but bad weather prevented this, and the RAF made the first attack at night. On 13/14 February some 796 Lancasters and nine Mosquitos attacked in two waves. The 244 No. 5 Group Lancasters struck first, dropping 800 tons of bombs with modest success, while the second wave (with Pathfinder support) proved more accurate, and its 1,800 tons of bombs created an immense firestorm, killing more than 50,000 people. USAAF B-17 and B-24 raids followed on 14 and 15 February, adding 700 tons of bombs to the total.

The sheer scale of destruction and death at Dresden shook many Allied observers, including Winston Churchill. On 28 March he penned a memo in which he observed:

It seems to me that the moment has come when the question of bombing German cities simply for the sake of increasing terror (though under other pretexts) should be reviewed, otherwise we shall come into control of an utterly ruined land. I feel the need for more precise concentration on military objectives, rather than mere acts of terror and wanton destruction, however impressive.

But Harris continued aiming for maximum destruction and maximum civilian casualties. Remaining targets had already been prioritised in such a way as to make this approach especially deadly. Operation *Thunderclap* continued on 14/15 February, when 499 Lancasters and 218 Halifaxes attacked Chemnitz (later Karl Marx Stadt), with rather less destructive results. Wesel, a small town on the Rhine close to the Allied front line, was then attacked daily between 16 and 19 February in an attempt to destroy its railway and road infrastructure.

Attacks on other cities, military targets and the oil industry continued unabated, with two of particular note. The raid on Essen on 11 March 1945 marked the largest number of aircraft despatched against a single target during the whole of the war. The 1,079 aircraft included 750 Lancasters, three of which were lost. The record was broken the following day when 1,108 aircraft, including 746 Lancasters, dropped a new high of 4,851 tons of bombs on Dortmund. Two Lancasters were lost.

By March 1945, however, a single raid could be enough to knock out a target. Würzburg had been spared for most of the war, not least because it contained only a single 'Priority 2' target, in the shape of a power switching station, and lacked 'Priority 1' targets. But under the new plans, it was a natural target, being easy to find and distinctive, with the town situated close to an autobahn and railway line. Finally, its narrow medieval streets made it almost a textbook target for incendiaries. Thus, when No. 5 Group despatched 226 Lancasters against the town on 16/17 March, Würzburg suffered 82 per cent destruction and 5,000 dead.

But the bombers did not have it all their own way.

On 3/4 March, 30 German intruders crossed the English coast and waited for the bombers returning from a raid on Ladbergen and mining operations off the Frisians. The Yorkshire-based Halifaxes suffered the heaviest losses that night, but eight Lancasters were also shot down, three of them returning from operations and five from training sorties.

The Luftwaffe could also sometimes meet the bombers in open combat. On 25 March, for example, during a No. 6 Group raid against Hannover, 30 Me 262 jets attacked the bombers, although only one Lancaster was lost, together with three Halifaxes that had been attacking Münster.

Three new Lancaster units joined Bomber Command's order of battle during March, comprising Nos 138, which joined No. 3 Group, and 427 and 429 Sqns, which replaced their Halifaxes within No. 6 Group. These were the last Lancaster units to see combat, since Nos 420 and 425 Sqns flew no operations after converting in April and May.

Just as it had attacked tactical and semi-tactical targets in support of the invasion of France, so too was Bomber Command pressed into service to support and prepare for the crossing of the Rhine. It mainly targeted important road and rail centres in the Rhineland and Ruhr, and among the first such targets was Pforzheim, a vital road and rail link that lay between Karlsruhe and Stuttgart. Bomber Command launched 362 Lancasters against the town on 23/24 February.

During the attack the No. 582 Sqn aircraft of Master Bomber Captain Edwin Swales, SAAF was badly hit, but he remained in the target area until satisfied that accuracy was good and the raid had achieved its objective. Swales stayed on station, directing the strike even after two night-fighter attacks had knocked out two engines and his rear guns. He then set course for France, remaining at the controls as his crew bailed out, before losing control of the crippled aircraft, in which he died. Swales won the VC for his cool heroism.

On 23 March, the very eve of the Rhine Crossing, No 5 Group despatched 77 Lancasters (led by Pathfinder Mosquitos) against Wesel, in concert with a massive artillery barrage. Allied troops had taken up position around the town and that night, 195 Lancasters made a second attack. Wesel was razed and taken without difficulty.

Among April's attacks, the 9/10th raid on Kiel by 591 Lancasters was notably impressive, with a very high concentration of bombs around the two designated aim points. It mainly targeted warships and U-boats, which were expected to make a run for Norway. The attack destroyed much port infrastructure and sunk 11 ships. *Admiral Scheer* was hit and capsized, while *Admiral Hipper* and *Emden* were badly damaged. Three Lancasters were lost.

Number 5 Group ended its offensive against the German communications network with an attack on the railway yards at Komotau, Czechoslovakia, on 18/19 April, all 114 of its Lancasters returning safely.

Five days before its surrender, and with British troops preparing a final push, 651 Lancasters, 100 Halifaxes and 16 Mosquitos attacked the port city of Bremen on 22 April. The Master Bomber called off the attack after 195 aircraft had bombed because smoke and dust had by then entirely obscured the target.

The last day of the war for the Lancaster force was 25 April 1945, when it attacked coastal gun batteries on the island of Wangerooge and Hitler's mountaintop retreat at Berchtesgaden. Some 158 Lancasters, 308 Halifaxes and 16 Mosquitos raided Wangerooge, while a slightly smaller force was despatched against Berchtesgaden. Although only 53 Lancasters of the 361 despatched pinpointed the primary target – Hitler's mountain retreat, known as the Berghof – it was totally destroyed, along with Göring's nearby residence, while the SS barracks were badly damaged.

On the night of 25/26 April, 107 Lancasters and 12 Mosquitos bombed an oil refinery at Vallo (Tonsberg), while four more mined Oslo Fjord. These were the Lancaster's last offensive missions.

Germany surrendered unconditionally on 7 May 1945. Bomber Command's casualty total of 55,000 dead was huge. A force that absorbed just seven per cent of Britain's military manpower had suffered a

quarter of the nation's war dead. Many of these men went to their deaths in the Lancaster.

MANNA AND *EXODUS*

The Lancaster ended the war on more peaceful missions. Operation *Manna* saw units conducting intensive food-dropping sorties to the starving Dutch populace between 28 April and 10 May, dropping 6,684 tons of food. Large areas of Holland were still under German control, but a truce was arranged with the local Wehrmacht commander and the Lancasters operated unmolested.

A veteran of the Dresden mission, No. 115 Sqn's HK696 had been despatched to Netheravon ten days after the controversial raid to develop and practise food dropping techniques. The RAF eventually settled on a low altitude delivery (from 200 to 500ft),

OPPOSITE Operation *Manna*: ground crew loading food supplies into slings for hoisting into the bomb bay of an Avro Lancaster of No. 514 Squadron RAF at Waterbeach, Cambridgeshire. (IWM © CH 15159)

dropping food from five bomb bay panniers at a speed of between 110 and 120kt, using half flap.

Operation *Exodus* began on 2 May, with large numbers of Lancasters ferrying PoWs home from Europe. Stripped and fitted with rudimentary seating for 25 passengers, the aircraft usually operated with a crew of six and flew 29,000 round trips, bringing home 74,000 ex-PoWs in 24 days. The operation was marred by the loss of a No. 514 Sqn aircraft, which crashed on take-off, killing everyone on board. Lancasters also ferried soldiers and other personnel home from Italy and the Mediterranean.

AFTER THE WAR

But this was far from the end of the Lancaster's RAF service. It served on until 1956 as a frontline maritime patrol and reconnaissance aircraft, leaving behind a legacy that continued with its Lincoln bomber and Shackleton anti-submarine and maritime patrol evolutions. Belatedly modified with radar for airborne early warning duties, the last of the Lancaster line, the

Shackleton AEW.Mk 2, entered service only in 1972 and soldiered on until 1991.

There were also the Lancastrian and York transport derivatives (the latter with an entirely new freighter fuselage), both of which played an important role in rebuilding Britain's post-war airline industry. They also delivered stalwart performance during the 1948–49 Berlin Airlift.

A number of ex-RAF Lancasters continued their military careers overseas. The Argentine and Egyptian air forces, and the French Navy, were the major operators, although the aircraft also flew search and rescue duties with the French government, and served in ones and twos with the Swedish, Soviet and Australian air arms.

Several Lancasters survived for display in museums in the UK and elsewhere. Offering a rather more involving experience, the Lincolnshire Aviation Heritage Centre offers taxi rides in its potentially airworthy Lancaster, while the Royal Air Force Battle of Britain Memorial Flight operates one of only two flying Lancasters extant. The other is with the Canadian Warplane Heritage Museum, and while the RAF's machine flies as a 'living' memorial to all those who have fallen in RAF service, the Canadian aircraft is also available for passenger experiences.

It is testament, if any were needed, to the greatness of the Lancaster that large sums of money and many hours of effort and expertise are poured into these few active airframes. The aircraft remains a spectacle in its own right, but it is important that it should remain flying to remind us of the sacrifice made by so many during World War II. As the RAF Battle of Britain Memorial Flight's motto so aptly states – Lest We Forget.

GLOSSARY

AA	Anti-aircraft	Flt Lt	Flight Lieutenant
ABC	Airborne Cigar	Flt Sgt	Flight Sergeant
AOC-in-C	Air Officer Commanding in Chief	FO	Flying Officer
CGM	Conspicuous Gallantry Medal	GP	General Purpose
CO	Commanding Officer	Gp Capt	Group Captain
DFC	Distinguished Flying Cross	HC	High Capacity
DFM	Distinguished Flying Medal	HE	High Explosive
DSO	Distinguished Service Order	IFF	Identification friend or foe
ECM	Electronic countermeasures	kt	Knot; one nautical mile per hour
EW	Electronic warfare	LAC	Leading Aircraftman
FE	Far East	MHz	megahertz
FIDO	Fog Investigation and Dispersal Operation	MU	Maintenance Unit
		OTU	Operational Training Unit
		PoW	Prisoner of war
		PRU	Photographic Reconnaissance Unit

OPPOSITE May 1944: British airmen load bombs onto a
Lancaster Bomber plane. (photo by Central Press/Gettyimages)

RAE	Royal Aircraft Establishment
RAF	Royal Air Force
RAAF	Royal Australian Air Force
RCAF	Royal Canadian Air Force
RNZAF	Royal New Zealand Air Force
SAAF	South African Air Force
SABS	Stabilised Automatic Bomb Sight
Sgt	Sergeant
SHAEF	Supreme Headquarters Allied Expeditionary Force
Sqn Ldr	Squadron Leader
USAAF	US Army Air Force
VC	Victoria Cross
Wg Cdr	Wing Commander
WO	Warrant Officer

First published in Great Britain in 2017 by Osprey Publishing,
PO Box 883, Oxford, OX1 9PL, UK
1385 Broadway, 5th Floor, New York, NY 10018, USA
E-mail: info@ospreypublishing.com

OSPREY PUBLISHING, PART OF BLOOMSBURY PUBLISHING PLC

In the compilation of this volume we relied on the following previously published
Osprey titles: COM 31 *Lancaster Squadrons 1942–43* and COM 35 *Lancaster
Squadrons 1944–45* by Jon Lake; DUE 51 *Bf110 vs Lancaster* by Robert
Forczyk; and AVG 21 *Avro Lancaster* by Richard Marks.

A CIP catalogue record for this book is available from the British Library.

ISBN: 9781472819390

PDF e-bookISBN: 9781472819406

ePub e-book ISBN: 9781472819413

Compiled by Paul E. Eden

Typeset in Sabon LT Std and Cleanwork.

Originated by PDQ Media, Bungay UK

Printed in China by C&C Offset Printing Co., Ltd.

17 18 19 20 21 10 9 8 7 6 5 4 3 2 1

ILLUSTRATIONS

Front cover: Artwork by Mark Postlethwaite (© Osprey Publishing)

Back cover: Profile artwork by Chris Davey (© Osprey Publishing)

Contents page: A restored Avro Lancaster bomber takes a run over Hamilton in
preparation for the Hamilton international Air Show June 17–18, 2008. (Photo
by Bernard Weil/Toronto Star via Getty Images)

Previous page: The crew of a Lancaster bomber walk away from their plane after
a flight while ground crew check it over, April 1943. (Photo by Fox Photos/Getty
Images)

Osprey Publishing supports the Woodland Trust, the UK's leading woodland
conservation charity. Between 2014 and 2018 our donations will be spent on
their Centenary Woods project in the UK.

To find out more about our authors and books visit **www.ospreypublishing.com**.
Here you will find extracts, author interviews, details of forthcoming events and
the option to sign up for our newsletter.